הגדה של פסח חידות אליהו

Haggadah
for the
Curious

MOSAICA PRESS

הגדה של פסח חידות אליהו

Haggadah
for the
Curious

Fascinating Ideas,
Questions, and Answers
for Teens and Adults

RABBI A. LEVIN

Mosaica Press, Inc.
© 2018 by Mosaica Press
Designed and typeset by Rayzel Broyde

ISBN-10: 1-946351-28-8
ISBN-13: 978-1-946351-28-9

Published and distributed by:
Mosaica Press, Inc.
www.mosaicapress.com
info@mosaicapress.com

לע״נ

רות בת אברהם

לע״נ

יוסף אהרן בן יצחק מיכל

„וְהִגַּדְתָּ לְבִנְךָ בַּיּוֹם הַהוּא לֵאמֹר
בַּעֲבוּר זֶה עָשָׂה ה' לִי בְּצֵאתִי מִמִּצְרָיִם" (שמות י"ג, ח)

לכבוד בנותינו היקרות

ליבא עדן נ"י
(Juliette Eden)

דפנה לאה נ"י
(Daphna Leah)

חנה נשמה נ"י
(Chloe Neshama)

ליילה נועה נ"י
(Laila Noa)

דוד הכהן ואריאלה בת-שבע מרקלין
זכרון יעקב, ישראל

David and Ariella Merklin
Zichron Yaakov, Israel

The following approbations appear in alphabetical order.

בס"ד

Rabbi Zev Leff   **הרב זאב לף**

Rabbi of Moshav Matityahu   מרא דאתרא מושב מתתיהו
Rosh HaYeshiva—Yeshiva Gedola Matityahu   ראש הישיבה—ישיבה גדולה מתתיהו

D.N. Modiin 71917   Tel: 08–976–1138 'טל   Fax: 08–976–5326 'פקס   71917 מודיעין .נ.ד

Dear Friends,

I have read portions of the manuscript *Haggadah for the Curious* by Rabbi Abba Levin. The author presents an abundance of interesting questions that illuminate the majority of the Pesach Haggadah. The questions are culled from many and varied Torah sources and reveal many aspects of the Seder that are not widely known. The style is interesting, enlightening, and entertaining and deals with both the halachic and hashkafic aspects of the Seder.

I recommend this very unique creation as a very effective companion to the Haggadah — a means to enhance one's Seder, making it more interesting to both children and adults, and a tool that will promote active interaction between the participants.

I commend Rabbi Levin, a former rabbinic student of mine, for a quality presentation and pray that Hashem bless him and his family with life and health and the wherewithal to continue to merit the community with further works.

Sincerely,
With Torah blessings,

Rabbi Zev Leff

תורה ומסורה
TORAH**UMESORAH**

May 24, 2017

To Whom It May Concern:

I am most pleased to share my very positive impression of Rabbi Abba Levin's new sefer on the Haggadah. The sefer contains interesting, concise and informative divrei Torah and knowledge about the Haggadah shel Pesach, and is presented in an easy and pleasant Q&A format.

I have known Rabbi Levin personally for a long time. He is a great talmid chochom who studied for many years in the Melbourne Kollel. For the past decade, he has been a successful Rebbi at the Yesodei HaTorah School in Melbourne.

Rabbi Levin's unassuming manner masks his brilliance. In addition to his vast knowledge of Torah, he is a most refined individual, of sterling character.

I trust that this sefer will be a very substantial and significant addition to one's Haggadah knowledge. I wish him continued hatzlacha in all his endeavors.

Sincerely,

Rabbi Dovid Nojowitz
National Director

400 MOUNT WILSON LANE • BALTIMORE, MARYLAND 21208

☎ 410.484.7200   🖶 410.484.3060   ✉ nirc@nirc.edu

Rabbi Beryl Weisbord
Menahel Ruchani

סיון תשע"ז

It is with great pleasure that I write these words of approbation for this new הגדה authored by our esteemed student Rabbi Abba Levin.

Rabbi Levin is an accomplished תלמיד חכם who is not only blessed with breadth of knowledge, but also with great clarity and depth of understanding as well.

This new הגדה is a product of the author's innovative thought process and passion to help our brothers and sisters grow in their עבודת השם. I'm confident that those who utilize this new הגדה will certainly reach greater heights in their קיום המצוה of סיפור יציאת מצרים.

With ברכות to our revered student and with תפלה that the new work find favor in the eyes of the entire Jewish community.

I remain,
Sincerely,

Rabbi Beryl Weisbord

KOLLEL BETH HATALMUD
YEHUDA FISHMAN INSTITUTE

כולל בית התלמוד
זכרון יהודה פישמאן

Herzog Community Centre ✤ Yaakov and Clara Lanzer Advanced Learning Program ✤ Rabbi Joseph and Stera Gutnick Study Hall ✤ Rodney and Lynda Adler Tape Library ✤ Yocheved Kaila a"h Bas R' Binyomin Zev Wurzburger Women's Program ✤ Tova Herszberg a"h Youth Foundation ✤ PLP University Program

בס"ד

Rabbi B Z Wurzburger Rosh HaKollel
Rabbi E Saftlas Menahel
Dr D Lanzer President
T (03) 9527 6156
F (03) 9527 8034

סידרי הכולל לכבוד יעקב וחיה לנצר
362a Carlisle St, Balaclava
Victoria 3183 Australia
@ office@kollel.com.au
W www.kollel.com.au

June 14, 2017

Rabbi Levin has been an outstanding member in our kollel for many years and is now a highly respected *mechanech* in Melbourne, who has greatly elevated the level of chinuch in our community and has acquired much acclaim for his role in developing and nurturing his talmidim with the love of Torah.

I have seen the manuscript *Haggadah for the Curious* and I was extremely impressed to see how the author masterfully makes the Haggadah come alive for young and old alike. This beautiful sefer is cleverly written in a light question and answer format, which encourages discussion and participation, in a lively, fun and creative manner. Through the many attention-grabbing riddles and challenges in this book, one's entire family will come to discover many fascinating and relatively unknown sources that shed light on the Haggadah, the laws and customs of Pesach, and the story of Yetzias Mitzrayim.

I wish Rabbi Levin much strength and success to produce many such inspirational works and to continue his *avodas hakodesh* in good health for many years to come.

With Torah blessings,

Rabbi Binyomin Wurzburger

Kollel Academy of Advanced Jewish Education Limited
ACN 005 628 035 -- ABN 94 005 628 035

TABLE OF CONTENTS

ACKNOWLEDGMENTS

First and foremost, my gratitude goes to *Hashem Yisbarach* for His unlimited kindness to me and my family, and for giving me the inspiration and ability to complete this Haggadah.

Word can't express the *hakaras hatov* I feel toward all my *rabbeim* for teaching me and always encouraging me to succeed. I wish to thank Cheder L'Yaldei Yeshurun (Copenhagen), Ner Israel Rabbinical College, Yeshivas Heichal HaTorah, Yeshivas Mir Yerushalayim, and Kollel Beth HaTalmud (Melbourne) for providing me with the opportunities to learn and grow in Torah and *avodas Hashem*. My appreciation also goes to Yeshivas Yesodei HaTorah (Melbourne) for granting me the privilege of teaching Torah to high school *talmidim* there over the last nine years.

Special thanks go to David and Ariella Merklin for dedicating this Haggadah, and to all the people who contributed to help make this Haggadah a reality. I also want to thank Kollel Beth HaTalmud and the Rosh HaKollel, Rabbi Wurzburger, for their support of this project.

My appreciation goes to the *Otzros HaHaggadah* (Mesivta) for providing the sources for many of the halachic questions and answers in this Haggadah.

Special thanks to Rav Yaacov Haber and Rabbi Doron Kornbluth and the entire staff at Mosaica Press for seeing this project to fruition—and for doing it in such a skilled and professional manner.

I appreciate all the kindness that has been bestowed upon us by my mother, sisters, and their families. Likewise, a special thank you goes to my parents-in-law, Rabbi and Mrs. Sofer, and all their children for always being there for us.

Above all, my appreciation goes to my wife for her outstanding devotion to our family in the most impressive way. Thank you for everything you do!

This Haggadah is dedicated *l'iluy nishmas* my late father, Leonard Levin, אליהו בן אבא הלוי, who left this world 15 Cheshvan 2009. I have fond memories of my father's Seder, and of how he would recite the Haggadah with special affection.

ערב חג הפסח תשע"ח

A. Levin

Melbourne, Australia

Feedback and comments can be sent to alevin@yht.vic.edu.au

INTRODUCTION

There is a central mitzvah that we fulfill on the night of the Seder and that is the mitzvah of סִפּוּר יְצִיאַת מִצְרַיִם, *recounting the story of the Exodus*. Besides reading the basic text of the Haggadah, we know that כָּל הַמַּרְבֶּה הֲרֵי זֶה מְשׁוּבָּח, *the more one talks about it, the better it is*. This can be accomplished in two ways: by delving into the miracles and events that took place during the actual redemption of the Jewish people (*Rambam, Chametz U'Matzah* 7:1–2) and by studying halachos pertinent to Pesach (*Tosefta Pesachim* 10:8; both opinions are codified in *Shulchan Aruch* 481:2). This Haggadah provides in greater detail both interesting material regarding the events of the Exodus as well as the halachos covering the Seder night.

The format of the Haggadah is in a manner of דֶּרֶךְ שְׁאֵילָה וּתְשׁוּבָה, question and answer. Following the theme of the evening, we encourage the children to ask questions, and we do a lot of things on the night of the Seder to stimulate them to ask. Rav Chaim Shmuelevitz (*Sichos Mussar*, p. 284) explains that it is only when one is bothered by the question that he will appreciate the answer. In this vein, the challenging questions and riddles in this book are intended to stimulate thought and discussion, and they will hopefully provide answers that will be appreciated by the readers and ultimately shared around the table.

This Haggadah does not contain the basic questions and answers that one would find in many other commentaries on the Haggadah since it

is intended for people who already have the rudimentary knowledge and are ready to add a new dimension to their Seder, both in terms of halachah and of recounting the miracles that occurred. For this reason, the questions herein are a little more challenging, but they are designed in such a manner as to engage the listener, who will want to hear the answer. This unique approach allows participants to share insights with family and friends in a way that will capture their attention.

An important point to note is that many different opinions are quoted in this volume, and while those opinions may be the right answer for the particular questions asked, it is not necessarily the accepted halachah or custom. It is therefore crucial to bear in mind that none of these answers should be relied upon for practical halachah. Wherever possible, we have attempted to clarify what the accepted halachah is based upon the rulings of the *Mishnah Berurah*.

Taking the time to prepare these challenges before the Seder is ideal, as it allows you to become familiar with the questions and answers and choose which to present at your table. Additionally, your familiarity with the material will enhance the experience for everyone at your Seder. Please note that these riddles also lend themselves to appropriate *divrei Torah* for the rest of the *yom tov* meals over the course of Pesach.

Enjoy!

בדיקת חמץ

On the night of the fourteenth of Nissan, a search for chametz is conducted by the light of a candle. Before the search, the following blessing is recited:

בָּרוּךְ אַתָּה יהוה אֱלֹהֵינוּ מֶלֶךְ הָעוֹלָם, אֲשֶׁר קִדְּשָׁנוּ בְּמִצְוֹתָיו, וְצִוָּנוּ עַל בִּעוּר חָמֵץ:

Conversation not relating to the search should be avoided until the search is completed.

After the search, the following declaration of nullification is made:

כָּל חֲמִירָא וַחֲמִיעָא דְּאִכָּא בִרְשׁוּתִי, דְּלָא חֲמִתֵּהּ, וּדְלָא בִעַרְתֵּהּ, וּדְלָא יְדַעְנָא לֵיהּ, לִבָּטֵל וְלֶהֱוֵי הֶפְקֵר כְּעַפְרָא דְאַרְעָא:

ביעור חמץ

The chametz is burned on the morning of the fourteenth of Nissan, before the end of the fifth hour of daylight.

After burning the chametz, the following declaration is made:

כָּל חֲמִירָא וַחֲמִיעָא דְּאִכָּא בִרְשׁוּתִי, דְּחֲזִתֵּהּ וּדְלָא חֲזִתֵּהּ, דְּחֲמִתֵּהּ וּדְלָא חֲמִתֵּהּ, דְּבִעַרְתֵּהּ וּדְלָא בִעַרְתֵּהּ, לִבָּטֵל וְלֶהֱוֵי הֶפְקֵר כְּעַפְרָא דְאַרְעָא:

What do chametz and avodah zarah (idol worship) have in common?

1. Both are *assur* to own.

2. Both must be burned.

3. One is not allowed to derive any benefit from either of them.

THE SEARCH FOR CHAMETZ

On the night of the fourteenth of Nissan, a search for chametz is conducted by the light of a candle. Before the search, the following blessing is recited:

Blessed are You, Hashem, our God, King of the universe, who has sanctified us with His commandments, and commanded us concerning the removal of chametz.

Conversation not relating to the search should be avoided until the search is completed.

After the search, the following declaration of nullification is made:

All leaven and chametz that is in my possession, which I have not seen nor disposed of, and about which I am unaware, is hereby nullified, and shall be ownerless as the dust of the earth.

BURNING THE CHAMETZ

The chametz is burned on the morning of the fourteenth of Nissan, before the end of the fifth hour of daylight.

After burning the chametz, the following declaration is made:

All leaven and chametz that is in my possession, whether I have seen it or not, whether I have disposed of it or not, is hereby nullified, and shall be ownerless as the dust of the earth.

4. These prohibitions extend to even the smallest amount (בְּמַשֶּׁהוּ).

5. One can do *bittul* on them.

6. One must search for them (see *Sifrei Re'eh* 61).

As we can see, there are many parallels between chametz and *avodah zarah* (see *Ba'al HaTurim, Shemos* 23:14–15). We also find that a sacrifice to an *avodah zarah* would often be accompanied with chametz bread (*Amos* 4:5).

סדר אמירת קרבן פסח

Following Minchah, many people have the custom to recite the verses which relate to the bringing of the Pesach offering.

רִבּוֹן הָעוֹלָמִים, אַתָּה צִוִּיתָנוּ לְהַקְרִיב קָרְבַּן הַפֶּסַח בְּמוֹעֲדוֹ בְּאַרְבָּעָה עָשָׂר יוֹם לַחֹדֶשׁ הָרִאשׁוֹן, וְלִהְיוֹת כֹּהֲנִים בַּעֲבוֹדָתָם וּלְוִיִּם בְּדוּכָנָם וְיִשְׂרָאֵל בְּמַעֲמָדָם קוֹרְאִים אֶת הַהַלֵּל. וְעַתָּה בַּעֲוֹנוֹתֵינוּ חָרַב בֵּית הַמִּקְדָשׁ וּבָטַל קָרְבַּן הַפֶּסַח, וְאֵין לָנוּ לֹא כֹהֵן בַּעֲבוֹדָתוֹ וְלֹא לֵוִי בְּדוּכָנוֹ וְלֹא יִשְׂרָאֵל בְּמַעֲמָדוֹ, וְלֹא נוּכַל לְהַקְרִיב הַיּוֹם קָרְבַּן פֶּסַח. אֲבָל אַתָּה אָמַרְתָּ וּנְשַׁלְּמָה פָרִים שְׂפָתֵינוּ. לָכֵן יְהִי רָצוֹן מִלְּפָנֶיךָ יְיָ אֱלֹהֵינוּ וֵאלֹהֵי אֲבוֹתֵינוּ שֶׁיִּהְיֶה שִׂיחַ שִׂפְתוֹתֵינוּ חָשׁוּב לְפָנֶיךָ כְּאִלּוּ הִקְרַבְנוּ אֶת הַפֶּסַח בְּמוֹעֲדוֹ וְעָמַדְנוּ עַל מַעֲמָדוֹ, וְדִבְּרוּ הַלְוִיִּם בְּשִׁיר וְהַלֵּל לְהוֹדוֹת לַיְיָ. וְאַתָּה תְּכוֹנֵן מִקְדָּשֶׁךָ עַל מְכוֹנוֹ, וְנַעֲשֶׂה וְנַקְרִיב לְפָנֶיךָ אֶת הַפֶּסַח בְּמוֹעֲדוֹ, כְּמוֹ שֶׁכָּתַבְתָּ עָלֵינוּ בְּתוֹרָתֶךָ עַל יְדֵי מֹשֶׁה עַבְדֶּךָ כָּאָמוּר:

שמות יב:א–יא

וַיֹּאמֶר יְהֹוָה אֶל מֹשֶׁה וְאֶל אַהֲרֹן בְּאֶרֶץ מִצְרַיִם לֵאמֹר: הַחֹדֶשׁ הַזֶּה לָכֶם רֹאשׁ חֳדָשִׁים רִאשׁוֹן הוּא לָכֶם לְחָדְשֵׁי הַשָּׁנָה: דַּבְּרוּ אֶל כָּל עֲדַת יִשְׂרָאֵל לֵאמֹר בֶּעָשֹׂר לַחֹדֶשׁ הַזֶּה וְיִקְחוּ לָהֶם אִישׁ שֶׂה לְבֵית אָבֹת שֶׂה לַבָּיִת: וְאִם יִמְעַט הַבַּיִת מִהְיֹת מִשֶּׂה וְלָקַח הוּא וּשְׁכֵנוֹ הַקָּרֹב אֶל בֵּיתוֹ בְּמִכְסַת נְפָשֹׁת אִישׁ לְפִי אָכְלוֹ תָּכֹסּוּ עַל הַשֶּׂה: שֶׂה תָמִים זָכָר בֶּן שָׁנָה יִהְיֶה לָכֶם מִן

The *Korban Pesach* was slaughtered in Mitzrayim in order to demonstrate that *Bnei Yisrael* no longer had any connection to the *avodah zarah* of the Egyptians (who regarded sheep as a god). It stands to reason that the prohibition of chametz on Pesach also serves as a reminder to stay clear from those idolatrous practices. Since chametz is closely linked to *avodah zarah*, we can understand why the Torah is so strict on removing every little trace of it from our possessions. For one week a year, we receive a "refresher course" in *emunah*, and it requires us to separate from all areas of *avodah zarah*. Since chametz was used in conjunction with *avodah zarah*, we have been commanded to distance ourselves from it on Pesach (see *Haggadah Sheleimah*, p. 221).

הַכְּבָשִׂים וּמִן הָעִזִּים תִּקָּחוּ: וְהָיָה לָכֶם לְמִשְׁמֶרֶת עַד אַרְבָּעָה עָשָׂר יוֹם לַחֹדֶשׁ הַזֶּה וְשָׁחֲטוּ אֹתוֹ כֹּל קְהַל עֲדַת יִשְׂרָאֵל בֵּין הָעַרְבָּיִם: וְלָקְחוּ מִן הַדָּם וְנָתְנוּ עַל שְׁתֵּי הַמְּזוּזֹת וְעַל הַמַּשְׁקוֹף עַל הַבָּתִּים אֲשֶׁר יֹאכְלוּ אֹתוֹ בָּהֶם: וְאָכְלוּ אֶת הַבָּשָׂר בַּלַּיְלָה הַזֶּה צְלִי אֵשׁ וּמַצּוֹת עַל מְרֹרִים יֹאכְלֻהוּ: אַל תֹּאכְלוּ מִמֶּנּוּ נָא וּבָשֵׁל מְבֻשָּׁל בַּמָּיִם כִּי אִם צְלִי אֵשׁ רֹאשׁוֹ עַל כְּרָעָיו וְעַל קִרְבּוֹ: וְלֹא תוֹתִירוּ מִמֶּנּוּ עַד בֹּקֶר וְהַנֹּתָר מִמֶּנּוּ עַד בֹּקֶר בָּאֵשׁ תִּשְׂרֹפוּ: וְכָכָה תֹּאכְלוּ אֹתוֹ מָתְנֵיכֶם חֲגֻרִים נַעֲלֵיכֶם בְּרַגְלֵיכֶם וּמַקֶּלְכֶם בְּיֶדְכֶם וַאֲכַלְתֶּם אֹתוֹ בְּחִפָּזוֹן פֶּסַח הוּא לַיהוָה:

שמות יב:כא-כח

וַיִּקְרָא מֹשֶׁה לְכָל זִקְנֵי יִשְׂרָאֵל וַיֹּאמֶר אֲלֵהֶם מִשְׁכוּ וּקְחוּ לָכֶם צֹאן לְמִשְׁפְּחֹתֵיכֶם וְשַׁחֲטוּ הַפָּסַח: וּלְקַחְתֶּם אֲגֻדַּת אֵזוֹב וּטְבַלְתֶּם בַּדָּם אֲשֶׁר בַּסַּף וְהִגַּעְתֶּם אֶל הַמַּשְׁקוֹף וְאֶל שְׁתֵּי הַמְּזוּזֹת מִן הַדָּם אֲשֶׁר בַּסַּף וְאַתֶּם לֹא תֵצְאוּ אִישׁ מִפֶּתַח בֵּיתוֹ עַד בֹּקֶר: וְעָבַר יְהוָה לִנְגֹּף אֶת מִצְרַיִם וְרָאָה אֶת הַדָּם עַל הַמַּשְׁקוֹף וְעַל שְׁתֵּי הַמְּזוּזֹת וּפָסַח יְהוָה עַל הַפֶּתַח וְלֹא יִתֵּן הַמַּשְׁחִית לָבֹא אֶל בָּתֵּיכֶם לִנְגֹּף: וּשְׁמַרְתֶּם אֶת הַדָּבָר הַזֶּה לְחָק לְךָ וּלְבָנֶיךָ עַד עוֹלָם: וְהָיָה כִּי תָבֹאוּ אֶל הָאָרֶץ אֲשֶׁר יִתֵּן יְהוָה לָכֶם כַּאֲשֶׁר דִּבֵּר וּשְׁמַרְתֶּם אֶת הָעֲבֹדָה הַזֹּאת: וְהָיָה כִּי יֹאמְרוּ אֲלֵיכֶם בְּנֵיכֶם מָה הָעֲבֹדָה הַזֹּאת לָכֶם: וַאֲמַרְתֶּם זֶבַח פֶּסַח הוּא לַיהוָה אֲשֶׁר פָּסַח עַל בָּתֵּי בְנֵי יִשְׂרָאֵל בְּמִצְרַיִם בְּנָגְפּוֹ אֶת מִצְרַיִם וְאֶת בָּתֵּינוּ הִצִּיל וַיִּקֹּד הָעָם וַיִּשְׁתַּחֲווּ: וַיֵּלְכוּ וַיַּעֲשׂוּ בְּנֵי יִשְׂרָאֵל כַּאֲשֶׁר צִוָּה יְהוָה אֶת מֹשֶׁה וְאַהֲרֹן כֵּן עָשׂוּ:

שמות יב:מג-נ

וַיֹּאמֶר יְהוָה אֶל מֹשֶׁה וְאַהֲרֹן זֹאת חֻקַּת הַפָּסַח כָּל בֶּן נֵכָר לֹא יֹאכַל בּוֹ: וְכָל עֶבֶד אִישׁ מִקְנַת כָּסֶף וּמַלְתָּה אֹתוֹ אָז יֹאכַל בּוֹ: תּוֹשָׁב וְשָׂכִיר לֹא יֹאכַל בּוֹ: בְּבַיִת אֶחָד יֵאָכֵל לֹא תוֹצִיא מִן הַבַּיִת מִן הַבָּשָׂר חוּצָה וְעֶצֶם לֹא תִשְׁבְּרוּ בוֹ: כָּל עֲדַת יִשְׂרָאֵל יַעֲשׂוּ אֹתוֹ: וְכִי יָגוּר אִתְּךָ גֵּר וְעָשָׂה פֶסַח לַיהוָה הִמּוֹל לוֹ כָל זָכָר וְאָז יִקְרַב לַעֲשֹׂתוֹ וְהָיָה כְּאֶזְרַח הָאָרֶץ וְכָל עָרֵל לֹא יֹאכַל בּוֹ: תּוֹרָה אַחַת יִהְיֶה לָאֶזְרָח וְלַגֵּר הַגָּר בְּתוֹכְכֶם: וַיַּעֲשׂוּ כָּל בְּנֵי יִשְׂרָאֵל כַּאֲשֶׁר צִוָּה יְהוָה אֶת מֹשֶׁה וְאֶת אַהֲרֹן כֵּן עָשׂוּ:

ויקרא כג:ד-ה

אֵלֶּה מוֹעֲדֵי יְהוָה מִקְרָאֵי קֹדֶשׁ אֲשֶׁר תִּקְרְאוּ אֹתָם בְּמוֹעֲדָם: בַּחֹדֶשׁ הָרִאשׁוֹן בְּאַרְבָּעָה עָשָׂר לַחֹדֶשׁ בֵּין הָעַרְבָּיִם פֶּסַח לַיהוָה:

במדבר ט:א-יד

וַיְדַבֵּר יְהוָה אֶל מֹשֶׁה בְמִדְבַּר סִינַי בַּשָּׁנָה הַשֵּׁנִית לְצֵאתָם מֵאֶרֶץ מִצְרַיִם בַּחֹדֶשׁ הָרִאשׁוֹן לֵאמֹר: וְיַעֲשׂוּ בְנֵי יִשְׂרָאֵל אֶת הַפָּסַח בְּמוֹעֲדוֹ: בְּאַרְבָּעָה עָשָׂר יוֹם

בַּחֹדֶשׁ הַזֶּה בֵּין הָעַרְבַּיִם תַּעֲשׂוּ אֹתוֹ בְּמוֹעֲדוֹ כְּכָל חֻקֹּתָיו וּכְכָל מִשְׁפָּטָיו תַּעֲשׂוּ אֹתוֹ: וַיְדַבֵּר מֹשֶׁה אֶל בְּנֵי יִשְׂרָאֵל לַעֲשֹׂת הַפָּסַח: וַיַּעֲשׂוּ אֶת הַפֶּסַח בָּרִאשׁוֹן בְּאַרְבָּעָה עָשָׂר יוֹם לַחֹדֶשׁ בֵּין הָעַרְבַּיִם בְּמִדְבַּר סִינַי כְּכָל אֲשֶׁר צִוָּה יְהוָה אֶת מֹשֶׁה כֵּן עָשׂוּ בְּנֵי יִשְׂרָאֵל: וַיְהִי אֲנָשִׁים אֲשֶׁר הָיוּ טְמֵאִים לְנֶפֶשׁ אָדָם וְלֹא יָכְלוּ לַעֲשֹׂת הַפֶּסַח בַּיּוֹם הַהוּא וַיִּקְרְבוּ לִפְנֵי מֹשֶׁה וְלִפְנֵי אַהֲרֹן בַּיּוֹם הַהוּא: וַיֹּאמְרוּ הָאֲנָשִׁים הָהֵמָּה אֵלָיו אֲנַחְנוּ טְמֵאִים לְנֶפֶשׁ אָדָם לָמָּה נִגָּרַע לְבִלְתִּי הַקְרִיב אֶת קָרְבַּן יְהוָה בְּמֹעֲדוֹ בְּתוֹךְ בְּנֵי יִשְׂרָאֵל: וַיֹּאמֶר אֲלֵהֶם מֹשֶׁה עִמְדוּ וְאֶשְׁמְעָה מַה יְצַוֶּה יְהוָה לָכֶם:

וַיְדַבֵּר יְהוָה אֶל מֹשֶׁה לֵּאמֹר: דַּבֵּר אֶל בְּנֵי יִשְׂרָאֵל לֵאמֹר אִישׁ אִישׁ כִּי יִהְיֶה טָמֵא לָנֶפֶשׁ אוֹ בְדֶרֶךְ רְחֹקָה לָכֶם אוֹ לְדֹרֹתֵיכֶם וְעָשָׂה פֶסַח לַיהוָה: בַּחֹדֶשׁ הַשֵּׁנִי בְּאַרְבָּעָה עָשָׂר יוֹם בֵּין הָעַרְבַּיִם יַעֲשׂוּ אֹתוֹ עַל מַצּוֹת וּמְרֹרִים יֹאכְלֻהוּ: לֹא יַשְׁאִירוּ מִמֶּנּוּ עַד בֹּקֶר וְעֶצֶם לֹא יִשְׁבְּרוּ בוֹ כְּכָל חֻקַּת הַפֶּסַח יַעֲשׂוּ אֹתוֹ: וְהָאִישׁ אֲשֶׁר הוּא טָהוֹר וּבְדֶרֶךְ לֹא הָיָה וְחָדַל לַעֲשׂוֹת הַפֶּסַח וְנִכְרְתָה הַנֶּפֶשׁ הַהִוא מֵעַמֶּיהָ כִּי קָרְבַּן יְהוָה לֹא הִקְרִיב בְּמֹעֲדוֹ חֶטְאוֹ יִשָּׂא הָאִישׁ הַהוּא: וְכִי יָגוּר אִתְּכֶם גֵּר וְעָשָׂה פֶסַח לַיהוָה כְּחֻקַּת הַפֶּסַח וּכְמִשְׁפָּטוֹ כֵּן יַעֲשֶׂה חֻקָּה אַחַת יִהְיֶה לָכֶם וְלַגֵּר וּלְאֶזְרַח הָאָרֶץ:

במדבר כח:טז

וּבַחֹדֶשׁ הָרִאשׁוֹן בְּאַרְבָּעָה עָשָׂר יוֹם לַחֹדֶשׁ פֶּסַח לַיהוָה:

דברים טז:א-ח

שָׁמוֹר אֶת חֹדֶשׁ הָאָבִיב וְעָשִׂיתָ פֶּסַח לַיהוָה אֱלֹהֶיךָ כִּי בְּחֹדֶשׁ הָאָבִיב הוֹצִיאֲךָ יְהוָה אֱלֹהֶיךָ מִמִּצְרַיִם לָיְלָה: וְזָבַחְתָּ פֶּסַח לַיהוָה אֱלֹהֶיךָ צֹאן וּבָקָר בַּמָּקוֹם אֲשֶׁר יִבְחַר יְהוָה לְשַׁכֵּן שְׁמוֹ שָׁם: לֹא תֹאכַל עָלָיו חָמֵץ שִׁבְעַת יָמִים תֹּאכַל עָלָיו מַצּוֹת לֶחֶם עֹנִי כִּי בְחִפָּזוֹן יָצָאתָ מֵאֶרֶץ מִצְרַיִם לְמַעַן תִּזְכֹּר אֶת יוֹם צֵאתְךָ מֵאֶרֶץ מִצְרַיִם כֹּל יְמֵי חַיֶּיךָ: וְלֹא יֵרָאֶה לְךָ שְׂאֹר בְּכָל גְּבֻלְךָ שִׁבְעַת יָמִים וְלֹא יָלִין מִן הַבָּשָׂר אֲשֶׁר תִּזְבַּח בָּעֶרֶב בַּיּוֹם הָרִאשׁוֹן לַבֹּקֶר: לֹא תוּכַל לִזְבֹּחַ אֶת הַפָּסַח בְּאַחַד שְׁעָרֶיךָ אֲשֶׁר יְהוָה אֱלֹהֶיךָ נֹתֵן לָךְ: כִּי אִם אֶל הַמָּקוֹם אֲשֶׁר יִבְחַר יְהוָה אֱלֹהֶיךָ לְשַׁכֵּן שְׁמוֹ שָׁם תִּזְבַּח אֶת הַפֶּסַח בָּעֶרֶב כְּבוֹא הַשֶּׁמֶשׁ מוֹעֵד צֵאתְךָ מִמִּצְרָיִם: וּבִשַּׁלְתָּ וְאָכַלְתָּ בַּמָּקוֹם אֲשֶׁר יִבְחַר יְהוָה אֱלֹהֶיךָ בּוֹ וּפָנִיתָ בַבֹּקֶר וְהָלַכְתָּ לְאֹהָלֶיךָ: שֵׁשֶׁת יָמִים תֹּאכַל מַצּוֹת וּבַיּוֹם הַשְּׁבִיעִי עֲצֶרֶת לַיהוָה אֱלֹהֶיךָ לֹא תַעֲשֶׂה מְלָאכָה:

יהושע ה: י-יא

וַיַּחֲנוּ בְנֵי יִשְׂרָאֵל בַּגִּלְגָּל וַיַּעֲשׂוּ אֶת הַפֶּסַח בְּאַרְבָּעָה עָשָׂר יוֹם לַחֹדֶשׁ בָּעֶרֶב בְּעַרְבוֹת יְרִיחוֹ: וַיֹּאכְלוּ מֵעֲבוּר הָאָרֶץ מִמָּחֳרַת הַפֶּסַח מַצּוֹת וְקָלוּי בְּעֶצֶם הַיּוֹם הַזֶּה:

וַיְצַו הַמֶּלֶךְ אֶת כָּל הָעָם לֵאמֹר עֲשׂוּ פֶסַח לַיהוָה אֱלֹהֵיכֶם כַּכָּתוּב עַל סֵפֶר
הַבְּרִית הַזֶּה: כִּי לֹא נַעֲשָׂה כַּפֶּסַח הַזֶּה מִימֵי הַשֹּׁפְטִים אֲשֶׁר שָׁפְטוּ אֶת יִשְׂרָאֵל
וְכֹל יְמֵי מַלְכֵי יִשְׂרָאֵל וּמַלְכֵי יְהוּדָה: כִּי אִם בִּשְׁמֹנֶה עֶשְׂרֵה שָׁנָה לַמֶּלֶךְ יֹאשִׁיָּהוּ
נַעֲשָׂה הַפֶּסַח הַזֶּה לַיהוָה בִּירוּשָׁלָ͏ִם:

דברי הימים ב ל:א-כ

וַיִּשְׁלַח יְחִזְקִיָּהוּ עַל כָּל יִשְׂרָאֵל וִיהוּדָה וְגַם אִגְּרוֹת כָּתַב עַל אֶפְרַיִם וּמְנַשֶּׁה
לָבוֹא לְבֵית יְהוָה בִּירוּשָׁלַ͏ִם לַעֲשׂוֹת פֶּסַח לַיהוָה אֱלֹהֵי יִשְׂרָאֵל: וַיִּוָּעַץ הַמֶּלֶךְ
וְשָׂרָיו וְכָל הַקָּהָל בִּירוּשָׁלָ͏ִם לַעֲשׂוֹת הַפֶּסַח בַּחֹדֶשׁ הַשֵּׁנִי: כִּי לֹא יָכְלוּ לַעֲשֹׂתוֹ
בָּעֵת הַהִיא כִּי הַכֹּהֲנִים לֹא הִתְקַדְּשׁוּ לְמַדַּי וְהָעָם לֹא נֶאֶסְפוּ לִירוּשָׁלָ͏ִם: וַיִּישַׁר
הַדָּבָר בְּעֵינֵי הַמֶּלֶךְ וּבְעֵינֵי כָּל הַקָּהָל: וַיַּעֲמִידוּ דָבָר לְהַעֲבִיר קוֹל בְּכָל יִשְׂרָאֵל
מִבְּאֵר שֶׁבַע וְעַד דָּן לָבוֹא לַעֲשׂוֹת פֶּסַח לַיהוָה אֱלֹהֵי יִשְׂרָאֵל בִּירוּשָׁלָ͏ִם כִּי
לֹא לָרֹב עָשׂוּ כַּכָּתוּב: וַיֵּלְכוּ הָרָצִים בָּאִגְּרוֹת מִיַּד הַמֶּלֶךְ וְשָׂרָיו בְּכָל יִשְׂרָאֵל
וִיהוּדָה וּכְמִצְוַת הַמֶּלֶךְ לֵאמֹר בְּנֵי יִשְׂרָאֵל שׁוּבוּ אֶל יְהוָה אֱלֹהֵי אַבְרָהָם
יִצְחָק וְיִשְׂרָאֵל וְיָשֹׁב אֶל הַפְּלֵיטָה הַנִּשְׁאֶרֶת לָכֶם מִכַּף מַלְכֵי אַשּׁוּר: וְאַל
תִּהְיוּ כַּאֲבוֹתֵיכֶם וְכַאֲחֵיכֶם אֲשֶׁר מָעֲלוּ בַּיהוָה אֱלֹהֵי אֲבוֹתֵיהֶם וַיִּתְּנֵם לְשַׁמָּה
כַּאֲשֶׁר אַתֶּם רֹאִים: עַתָּה אַל תַּקְשׁוּ עָרְפְּכֶם כַּאֲבוֹתֵיכֶם תְּנוּ יָד לַיהוָה וּבֹאוּ
לְמִקְדָּשׁוֹ אֲשֶׁר הִקְדִּישׁ לְעוֹלָם וְעִבְדוּ אֶת יְהוָה אֱלֹהֵיכֶם וְיָשֹׁב מִכֶּם חֲרוֹן
אַפּוֹ: כִּי בְשׁוּבְכֶם עַל יְהוָה אֲחֵיכֶם וּבְנֵיכֶם לְרַחֲמִים לִפְנֵי שׁוֹבֵיהֶם וְלָשׁוּב
לָאָרֶץ הַזֹּאת כִּי חַנּוּן וְרַחוּם יְהוָה אֱלֹהֵיכֶם וְלֹא יָסִיר פָּנִים מִכֶּם אִם תָּשׁוּבוּ
אֵלָיו: וַיִּהְיוּ הָרָצִים עֹבְרִים מֵעִיר לָעִיר בְּאֶרֶץ אֶפְרַיִם וּמְנַשֶּׁה וְעַד זְבֻלוּן
וַיִּהְיוּ מַשְׂחִיקִים עֲלֵיהֶם וּמַלְעִגִים בָּם: אַךְ אֲנָשִׁים מֵאָשֵׁר וּמְנַשֶּׁה וּמִזְּבֻלוּן
נִכְנְעוּ וַיָּבֹאוּ לִירוּשָׁלָ͏ִם: גַּם בִּיהוּדָה הָיְתָה יַד הָאֱלֹהִים לָתֵת לָהֶם לֵב אֶחָד
לַעֲשׂוֹת מִצְוַת הַמֶּלֶךְ וְהַשָּׂרִים בִּדְבַר יְהוָה: וַיֵּאָסְפוּ יְרוּשָׁלַ͏ִם עַם רָב לַעֲשׂוֹת
אֶת חַג הַמַּצּוֹת בַּחֹדֶשׁ הַשֵּׁנִי קָהָל לָרֹב מְאֹד: וַיָּקֻמוּ וַיָּסִירוּ אֶת הַמִּזְבְּחוֹת
אֲשֶׁר בִּירוּשָׁלָ͏ִם וְאֵת כָּל הַמְקַטְּרוֹת הֵסִירוּ וַיַּשְׁלִיכוּ לְנַחַל קִדְרוֹן: וַיִּשְׁחֲטוּ
הַפֶּסַח בְּאַרְבָּעָה עָשָׂר לַחֹדֶשׁ הַשֵּׁנִי וְהַכֹּהֲנִים וְהַלְוִיִּם נִכְלְמוּ וַיִּתְקַדְּשׁוּ וַיָּבִיאוּ
עֹלוֹת בֵּית יְהוָה: וַיַּעַמְדוּ עַל עָמְדָם כְּמִשְׁפָּטָם כְּתוֹרַת מֹשֶׁה אִישׁ הָאֱלֹהִים
הַכֹּהֲנִים זֹרְקִים אֶת הַדָּם מִיַּד הַלְוִיִּם: כִּי רַבַּת בַּקָּהָל אֲשֶׁר לֹא הִתְקַדָּשׁוּ
וְהַלְוִיִּם עַל שְׁחִיטַת הַפְּסָחִים לְכֹל לֹא טָהוֹר לְהַקְדִּישׁ לַיהוָה: כִּי מַרְבִּית הָעָם
רַבַּת מֵאֶפְרַיִם וּמְנַשֶּׁה יִשָּׂשכָר וּזְבֻלוּן לֹא הִטֶּהָרוּ כִּי אָכְלוּ אֶת הַפֶּסַח בְּלֹא
כַכָּתוּב כִּי הִתְפַּלֵּל יְחִזְקִיָּהוּ עֲלֵיהֶם לֵאמֹר יְהוָה הַטּוֹב יְכַפֵּר בְּעַד: כָּל לְבָבוֹ
הֵכִין לִדְרוֹשׁ הָאֱלֹהִים יְהוָה אֱלֹהֵי אֲבוֹתָיו וְלֹא כְּטָהֳרַת הַקֹּדֶשׁ: וַיִּשְׁמַע יְהוָה
אֶל יְחִזְקִיָּהוּ וַיִּרְפָּא אֶת הָעָם:

וַיַּעַשׂ יֹאשִׁיָּהוּ בִירוּשָׁלַ͏ִם פֶּסַח לַיהֹוָה וַיִּשְׁחֲטוּ הַפֶּסַח בְּאַרְבָּעָה עָשָׂר לַחֹדֶשׁ
הָרִאשׁוֹן: וַיַּעֲמֵד הַכֹּהֲנִים עַל מִשְׁמְרוֹתָם וַיְחַזְּקֵם לַעֲבוֹדַת בֵּית יְהֹוָה: וַיֹּאמֶר
לַלְוִיִּם הַמְּבִינִים לְכׇל יִשְׂרָאֵל הַקְּדוֹשִׁים לַיהֹוָה תְּנוּ אֶת אֲרוֹן הַקֹּדֶשׁ בַּבַּיִת
אֲשֶׁר בָּנָה שְׁלֹמֹה בֶן דָּוִיד מֶלֶךְ יִשְׂרָאֵל אֵין לָכֶם מַשָּׂא בַּכָּתֵף עַתָּה עִבְדוּ
אֶת יְהֹוָה אֱלֹהֵיכֶם וְאֵת עַמּוֹ יִשְׂרָאֵל: וְהָכִינוּ לְבֵית אֲבוֹתֵיכֶם כְּמַחְלְקוֹתֵיכֶם
בִּכְתָב דָּוִיד מֶלֶךְ יִשְׂרָאֵל וּבְמִכְתַּב שְׁלֹמֹה בְנוֹ: וְעִמְדוּ בַקֹּדֶשׁ לִפְלֻגּוֹת בֵּית
הָאָבוֹת לַאֲחֵיכֶם בְּנֵי הָעָם וַחֲלֻקַּת בֵּית אָב לַלְוִיִּם: וְשַׁחֲטוּ הַפָּסַח וְהִתְקַדְּשׁוּ
וְהָכִינוּ לַאֲחֵיכֶם לַעֲשׂוֹת כִּדְבַר יְהֹוָה בְּיַד מֹשֶׁה: וַיָּרֶם יֹאשִׁיָּהוּ לִבְנֵי הָעָם
צֹאן כְּבָשִׂים וּבְנֵי עִזִּים הַכֹּל לַפְּסָחִים לְכׇל הַנִּמְצָא לְמִסְפַּר שְׁלֹשִׁים אֶלֶף
וּבָקָר שְׁלֹשֶׁת אֲלָפִים אֵלֶּה מֵרְכוּשׁ הַמֶּלֶךְ: וְשָׂרָיו לִנְדָבָה לָעָם לַכֹּהֲנִים
וְלַלְוִיִּם הֵרִימוּ חִלְקִיָּה וּזְכַרְיָהוּ וִיחִיאֵל נְגִידֵי בֵּית הָאֱלֹהִים לַכֹּהֲנִים נָתְנוּ
לַפְּסָחִים אַלְפַּיִם וְשֵׁשׁ מֵאוֹת וּבָקָר שְׁלֹשׁ מֵאוֹת: וְכָנַנְיָהוּ וּשְׁמַעְיָהוּ וּנְתַנְאֵל
אֶחָיו וַחֲשַׁבְיָהוּ וִיעִיאֵל וְיוֹזָבָד שָׂרֵי הַלְוִיִּם הֵרִימוּ לַלְוִיִּם לַפְּסָחִים חֲמֵשֶׁת
אֲלָפִים וּבָקָר חֲמֵשׁ מֵאוֹת: וַתִּכּוֹן הָעֲבוֹדָה וַיַּעַמְדוּ הַכֹּהֲנִים עַל עׇמְדָם
וְהַלְוִיִּם עַל מַחְלְקוֹתָם כְּמִצְוַת הַמֶּלֶךְ: וַיִּשְׁחֲטוּ הַפָּסַח וַיִּזְרְקוּ הַכֹּהֲנִים
מִיָּדָם וְהַלְוִיִּם מַפְשִׁיטִים: וַיָּסִירוּ הָעֹלָה לְתִתָּם לְמִפְלַגּוֹת לְבֵית אָבוֹת לִבְנֵי
הָעָם לְהַקְרִיב לַיהֹוָה כַּכָּתוּב בְּסֵפֶר מֹשֶׁה וְכֵן לַבָּקָר: וַיְבַשְּׁלוּ הַפֶּסַח בָּאֵשׁ
כַּמִּשְׁפָּט וְהַקֳּדָשִׁים בִּשְּׁלוּ בַּסִּירוֹת וּבַדְּוָדִים וּבַצֵּלָחוֹת וַיָּרִיצוּ לְכׇל בְּנֵי הָעָם:
וְאַחַר הֵכִינוּ לָהֶם וְלַכֹּהֲנִים כִּי הַכֹּהֲנִים בְּנֵי אַהֲרֹן בְּהַעֲלוֹת הָעוֹלָה וְהַחֲלָבִים
עַד לָיְלָה וְהַלְוִיִּם הֵכִינוּ לָהֶם וְלַכֹּהֲנִים בְּנֵי אַהֲרֹן: וְהַמְשֹׁרְרִים בְּנֵי אָסָף עַל
מַעֲמָדָם כְּמִצְוַת דָּוִיד וְאָסָף וְהֵימָן וִידֻתוּן חוֹזֵה הַמֶּלֶךְ וְהַשֹּׁעֲרִים לְשַׁעַר
וָשַׁעַר אֵין לָהֶם לָסוּר מֵעַל עֲבֹדָתָם כִּי אֲחֵיהֶם הַלְוִיִּם הֵכִינוּ לָהֶם: וַתִּכּוֹן
כׇּל עֲבוֹדַת יְהֹוָה בַּיּוֹם הַהוּא לַעֲשׂוֹת הַפֶּסַח וְהַעֲלוֹת עֹלוֹת עַל מִזְבַּח יְהֹוָה
כְּמִצְוַת הַמֶּלֶךְ יֹאשִׁיָּהוּ: וַיַּעֲשׂוּ בְנֵי יִשְׂרָאֵל הַנִּמְצְאִים אֶת הַפֶּסַח בָּעֵת הַהִיא
וְאֶת חַג הַמַּצּוֹת שִׁבְעַת יָמִים: וְלֹא נַעֲשָׂה פֶסַח כָּמֹהוּ בְּיִשְׂרָאֵל מִימֵי שְׁמוּאֵל
הַנָּבִיא וְכׇל מַלְכֵי יִשְׂרָאֵל לֹא עָשׂוּ כַּפֶּסַח אֲשֶׁר עָשָׂה יֹאשִׁיָּהוּ וְהַכֹּהֲנִים
וְהַלְוִיִּם וְכׇל יְהוּדָה וְיִשְׂרָאֵל הַנִּמְצָא וְיוֹשְׁבֵי יְרוּשָׁלָ͏ִם: בִּשְׁמוֹנֶה עֶשְׂרֵה שָׁנָה
לְמַלְכוּת יֹאשִׁיָּהוּ נַעֲשָׂה הַפֶּסַח הַזֶּה:

עירוב תבשילין

*When Pesach (or any festival) occurs on a Friday, an Eruv Tavshilin must be made in order
to allow cooking (and other preparations) for Shabbos on that Friday. The Eruv consists of
a whole piece of matzah and at least a kezayis (approximately the volume of half an egg) of
a cooked food, which are set aside (before the festival begins) and kept intact until Shabbos
preparations are completed. The Eruv is held in the hand, and the following blessing is recited:*

בָּרוּךְ אַתָּה יהוה אֱלֹהֵינוּ מֶלֶךְ הָעוֹלָם, אֲשֶׁר קִדְּשָׁנוּ
בְּמִצְוֹתָיו, וְצִוָּנוּ עַל מִצְוַת עֵרוּב:

Declaration of intent:

בְּהָדֵין עֵירוּבָא יְהֵא שָׁרֵא לָנָא לַאֲפוּיֵי וּלְבַשׁוּלֵי
וּלְאַטְמוּנֵי וּלְאַדְלוּקֵי שְׁרָגָא וּלְאַפּוּקֵי וּלְמֶעְבַּד כָּל
צָרְכָּנָא מִיּוֹמָא טָבָא לְשַׁבַּתָּא:

הדלקת הנרות

The blessings over the lighting of the holiday candles:

(On Shabbos, the words in parentheses are added.)

בָּרוּךְ אַתָּה יהוה אֱלֹהֵינוּ מֶלֶךְ הָעוֹלָם, אֲשֶׁר קִדְּשָׁנוּ
בְּמִצְוֹתָיו, וְצִוָּנוּ לְהַדְלִיק נֵר שֶׁל (שַׁבָּת וְשֶׁל) יוֹם טוֹב:
בָּרוּךְ אַתָּה יהוה אֱלֹהֵינוּ מֶלֶךְ הָעוֹלָם, שֶׁהֶחֱיָנוּ וְקִיְּמָנוּ
וְהִגִּיעָנוּ לַזְּמַן הַזֶּה:

ERUV TAVSHILIN

When Pesach (or any festival) occurs on a Friday, an Eruv Tavshilin must be made in order to allow cooking (and other preparations) for Shabbos on that Friday. The Eruv consists of a whole piece of matzah and at least a kezayis (approximately the volume of half an egg) of a cooked food, which are set aside (before the festival begins) and kept intact until Shabbos preparations are completed. The Eruv is held in the hand, and the following blessing is recited:

Blessed are You, Hashem, our God, King of the universe, Who has sanctified us through His commandments, and commanded us concerning the precept of the eruv.

Declaration of intent:

By this eruv it shall be permitted for us to bake, to cook, to insulate pots of hot food, to light candles, and to do all [permissible acts] that are necessary on the festival in preparation for the Sabbath.

LIGHTING THE CANDLES

The blessings over the lighting of the holiday candles:

(On Shabbos, the words in parentheses are added.)

Blessed are You, Hashem, our God, King of the universe, Who has sanctified us through His commandments, and commanded us to kindle the candle of (the Sabbath and) the festival.

Blessed are You, Hashem, our God, King of the universe, Who has granted us life and sustained us and allowed us to reach this occasion.

THE SEDER PLATE

Zero'a Beitzah

Maror

Karpas Charoses

Maror

Why would you place nuts and chocolates on the Seder plate?

In order to encourage the children to ask! (*Shibolei HaLeket* 218). The common *minhag* not to do so might be based on the *Kaf HaChaim* (473:58) that one should not add anything to the קְעָרָה other than what the Arizal said (*zero'a, beitzah, maror, charoses, karpas, chazeres* [for *Korech*] and the three matzos).

What mitzvah not performed on Pesach does the Seder plate hint to?

Work it out yourself: take each letter of the word קְעָרָה and switch it for the next letter in the *aleph-beis*, i.e., replace the ק with a ר, etc. Then, unscramble the letters to form a word for the mitzvah that is hinted to in the word קערה. This reminds us that already from Pesach we have to start preparing for the *Yamim Noraim* (*Devar Chaim* brought in *Otzros HaHaggadah*, p. 322).

Which item on the Seder plate are some people careful not to break?

The *zero'a*, because it's meant to remind us of the *Korban Pesach*, about which it says (12:46), וְעֶצֶם לֹא יִשְׁבְּרוּ בוֹ, *no bone should be broken from it* (*Kaf HaChaim* 473:60).

When might you be allowed to use dishes before they have been toiveled?

The *Mishnah Berurah* (472:6) writes that the Maharil would place the nice utensils that he had as collaterals from non-Jews on a special table to enjoy viewing them during the Seder. The Chasam Sofer adds (*Derashos* vol. 2, p. 255) that one is allowed on Seder night to use the collateral of a non-Jew even as a food utensil before it has been *toiveled*. The *kedushah* of Seder night in itself removes any traces of *tumah*, so one does not need to do *tevilas keilim* (this is not the common custom).

Who was the first person in history to use an idolater's collateral for the Seder?

In *Parashas Toldos*, we find that Rivkah Imeinu allowed Yaakov to use Eisav's clothes—without his knowledge!—to receive his father's *berachos*. This occurred on the first night of Pesach (*Rashi, Bereishis* 27:9). Thus, we have a precedent for the Maharil's ruling (*Chasam Sofer, Toras Moshe, Parashas Toldos*).

Can you prove that reclining is a Rabbinic mitzvah and not Torah-ordained?

The *Shulchan Aruch* writes (472:5) that a *talmid* in front of his *rebbi* is exempt from reclining. If reclining would be a mitzvah from the Torah, how could one be exempt from the mitzvah? It must be that it is only a Rabbinic mitzvah (see *Halichos Shlomo* 9:133).

Why, in fact, is a *talmid* in front of his *rebbi* exempt from reclining?

Reclining has to be דֶּרֶךְ חֵירוּת, in the manner of free men, and given that a *talmid* has a great measure of respect for his *rebbi*, he is unable to lean like a free man in front of his *rebbi*. Therefore, there is no requirement for the *talmid* to recline (Brisker Rav, *Haggadah Mi'Beis Levi*, p. 94).

Which man may decide on his own whether to recline or not?

While a *talmid* eating in front of his *rebbi* need not recline (*Shulchan Aruch* 472:5), if his *rebbi* gave him permission to, he has the option of

reclining if he wants to do so (*Aruch HaShulchan* 472:7). However, the *Mishnah Berurah* is of the opinion that, in this case, the student must recline (*Mishnah Berurah* 472:16).

Where does a halachah pertaining to women teach us the halachah for men?

The *She'iltos* (77) says that since it is not the normal way of women to recline, women are exempt from the requirement to do so. From here, the *Ra'aviyah* learned that in our times no one need recline, since today it's not the normal way of **anyone** to recline (*Bei'ur HaGra* 472:4). (For the practical halachah, see the *Rama* to 472:7.)

Which one person caused all the women at the Seder to be considered prominent?

The *Rama* writes (472:4), וְכָל הַנָּשִׁים שֶׁלָּנוּ מִקְרֵי חֲשׁוּבוֹת, *the women in our times are considered prominent* [and therefore should recline, as only prominent women have an obligation to recline (*Shulchan Aruch*, ibid.)]. This halachah can be traced back to Rabbeinu Gershom Me'or HaGolah, as he instituted that a man can't marry two women, and that a woman can't get divorced against her will. Therefore, women today are considered prominent (*Halichos Shlomo* 9:131).

When should one stay up late trying to understand riddles?

Many *Rishonim* composed poems of the *simanim*, detailing the steps of the Seder in poetic short language (the most well-known is *Kadesh, U'rechatz*, etc., but there are at least seventeen other versions still extant today). Reading these *simanim* only superficially would not be sufficient to properly understand them. In fact, the *simanim* were specifically composed in riddle form so that people would spend time attempting to understand what they refer to. This way, people were kept awake and busy on Seder night with matters relating to Pesach (*Shu"t Maharshal* 88).

———⊱ **Kaddesh** קדש ⊰———
Reciting Kiddush

———⊱ **Urchatz** ורחץ ⊰———
Washing the hands in preparation for Karpas

———⊱ **Karpas** כרפס ⊰———
Dipping a vegetable in salt water and eating it

———⊱ **Yachatz** יחץ ⊰———
Breaking the middle matzah

———⊱ **Maggid** מגיד ⊰———
Telling the story of the Exodus

———⊱ **Rachtzah** רחצה ⊰———
Washing the hands before the meal

———⊱ **Motzi** מוציא ⊰———
Reciting the Hamotzi blessing

———⊱ **Matzah** מצה ⊰———
Reciting the blessing over the matzah and eating it

———⊱ **Maror** מרור ⊰———
Eating the maror

———⊱ **Korech** כורך ⊰———
Eating a sandwich of matzah and maror

———⊱ **Shulchan Orech** שולחן עורך ⊰———
Eating the festive meal

———⊱ **Tzafun** צפון ⊰———
Eating the afikoman

———⊱ **Barech** ברך ⊰———
Reciting Birkas HaMazon

———⊱ **Hallel** הלל ⊰———
Reciting the remainder of Hallel

———⊱ **Nirtzah** נרצה ⊰———
Concluding the Seder with the hope that it was pleasing to Hashem!

קַדֵּשׁ

The first of the four cups of wine is poured. The leader should have another person pour the wine for him, as a gesture of leisure and freedom. There is, however, a widespread custom that all participants have another person pour for them. As he is about to recite Kiddush, one should bear in mind that he is about to fulfill the mitzvah of Kiddush and the mitzvah of the first of the four cups of wine.

On Friday night, the following paragraph is added:

וַיְהִי עֶרֶב וַיְהִי בֹקֶר

יוֹם הַשִּׁשִּׁי: וַיְכֻלּוּ הַשָּׁמַיִם וְהָאָרֶץ וְכָל צְבָאָם: וַיְכַל אֱלֹהִים בַּיּוֹם הַשְּׁבִיעִי מְלַאכְתּוֹ אֲשֶׁר עָשָׂה, וַיִּשְׁבֹּת בַּיּוֹם הַשְּׁבִיעִי מִכָּל מְלַאכְתּוֹ אֲשֶׁר עָשָׂה: וַיְבָרֶךְ אֱלֹהִים אֶת יוֹם הַשְּׁבִיעִי וַיְקַדֵּשׁ אֹתוֹ, כִּי בוֹ שָׁבַת מִכָּל מְלַאכְתּוֹ אֲשֶׁר בָּרָא אֱלֹהִים לַעֲשׂוֹת:

What is the connection between the four cups of wine and the four types of capital punishment?

The Rabbinic ordinance to drink four cups of wine was instituted to serve as a *kapparah* for one who violated any *aveirah* that would incur any of the four capital punishments (*Iyun Yaakov* to *Pesachim* 99b). Obviously, one would need to do *teshuvah* as well in order to receive a full *kapparah*, as without *teshuvah* there cannot be complete forgiveness. Perhaps wearing the *kittel* that we wear for the יָמִים נוֹרָאִים at the Seder also serves as a reminder to do *teshuvah* (Rav D. Merklin).

Which two things are done at the Seder to remember the plague of Blood?

It is preferable to use red wine on Seder night to remember the plague of Blood (*Pri Megadim* 472:13); likewise, the liquid texture of the *charoses* is a way to remember the plague of Blood (*Yerushalmi* 10:3 according to *P'nei Moshe*).

KADDESH

The first of the four cups of wine is poured. The leader should have another person pour the wine for him, as a gesture of leisure and freedom. There is, however, a widespread custom that all participants have another person pour for them. As he is about to recite Kiddush, one should bear in mind that he is about to fulfill the mitzvah of Kiddush and the mitzvah of the first of the four cups of wine.

On Friday night, the following paragraph is added:

And it was evening and it was morning, the sixth day.

The heavens and the earth and all their hosts were completed. God completed on the seventh day His work that He had done, and He rested on the seventh day from all His work that He had done. God blessed the seventh day and sanctified it, for on it He rested from all His work that God had created to make.

When does drinking a little make you want to drink more?

There are four expressions of redemption mentioned in the beginning of *Parashas Va'era* (6:6–7): וְהוֹצֵאתִי וְהִצַּלְתִּי וְגָאַלְתִּי וְלָקַחְתִּי, *I shall take you out, I shall rescue you, I shall redeem you, and I shall take you to Me for a people* (the commentators explain what each of the four expressions relate to). The Rabbinic ordinance of drinking four cups of wine is due to the four expressions of redemption mentioned in these *pesukim* (*Yerushalmi Pesachim* 10:1). Since the four terms of redemption express concepts, each higher than the other, the Rabbis could not institute that we eat four items of food or drink four types of regular drinks since, often, the more you eat or drink, the less you want to continue eating and drinking. There is one exception: wine—the more you drink, the more you enjoy it and want to drink more. This can help us appreciate that the four steps of the *geulah* came in ascending order. This is why *Chazal* instituted that we drink four cups of wine and nothing else (*Halichos Shlomo* 9:169).

סָבְרִי מָרָנָן וְרַבָּנָן וְרַבּוֹתַי

בָּרוּךְ אַתָּה יהוה אֱלֹהֵינוּ מֶלֶךְ הָעוֹלָם, בּוֹרֵא פְּרִי הַגָּפֶן:

בָּרוּךְ אַתָּה יהוה אֱלֹהֵינוּ מֶלֶךְ הָעוֹלָם, אֲשֶׁר בָּחַר בָּנוּ מִכָּל עָם, וְרוֹמְמָנוּ מִכָּל לָשׁוֹן, וְקִדְּשָׁנוּ בְּמִצְוֹתָיו, וַתִּתֶּן לָנוּ יהוה אֱלֹהֵינוּ בְּאַהֲבָה (שַׁבָּתוֹת לִמְנוּחָה וּ)מוֹעֲדִים לְשִׂמְחָה, חַגִּים וּזְמַנִּים לְשָׂשׂוֹן (אֶת יוֹם הַשַּׁבָּת הַזֶּה וְ)אֶת יוֹם חַג הַמַּצּוֹת הַזֶּה זְמַן חֵרוּתֵנוּ (בְּאַהֲבָה) מִקְרָא קֹדֶשׁ, זֵכֶר לִיצִיאַת מִצְרָיִם. כִּי בָנוּ בָחַרְתָּ וְאוֹתָנוּ קִדַּשְׁתָּ מִכָּל הָעַמִּים, (וְשַׁבָּת) וּמוֹעֲדֵי קָדְשֶׁךָ (בְּאַהֲבָה וּבְרָצוֹן) בְּשִׂמְחָה וּבְשָׂשׂוֹן הִנְחַלְתָּנוּ. בָּרוּךְ אַתָּה יהוה, מְקַדֵּשׁ (הַשַּׁבָּת וְ)יִשְׂרָאֵל וְהַזְּמַנִּים:

When is this the preferred order of the four cups: first, third, second?

One who does not have enough wine for the Seder should use what he has for Kiddush (the first cup); if he has more wine, he should use it for *Birkas Hamazon* (the third cup), as some say that *Birkas Hamazon* always requires a cup of wine; and if he has enough only for three cups, he should use the rest for the Haggadah (the second cup). The second cup precedes the fourth cup due to the principle of אֵין מַעֲבִירִין עַל הַמִּצְוֹת, *we do not jump over mitzvos*, and since the second cup comes before the fourth one, we therefore use

Blessed are You, Hashem, our God, King of the universe, Who creates the fruit of the vine.

BLESSED *are You, Hashem, our God, King of the universe, Who has chosen us from all the nations, and raised us above all nationalities, and made us holy through His commandments. You, Hashem, our God, gave us, with love, (Sabbaths for rest and) holidays for rejoicing, festivals and festive seasons for gladness—(this Sabbath day and) this day of the Festival of Matzos, the time of our freedom (with love), a holy convocation, in commemoration of the Exodus from Egypt. For You have chosen us and sanctified us from all the nations, and You have bestowed upon us Your holy (Sabbath and) festivals (with love and favor), with happiness and joy. Blessed are You, Hashem, Who sanctifies (the Sabbath and) Israel and the festive seasons.*

the remaining wine for the second cup (*Mishnah Berurah* 483:1, quoting the *Magen Avraham*).

What can one do at the Seder as a *segulah* to not need bitter medicines during the year?

One who pushes himself to drink the four cups of wine and eat the matzah and *afikoman* even though he finds it difficult will be spared from having to take bitter medicines throughout the year (*Orchos Chaim* 472:12, quoting *sefer Yafeh L'Lev*).

Who might be required to drink only two cups of wine at the Seder?

There is an opinion in the Midrash (*Shemos Rabbah* 6:4) that the four

On Saturday night, the following section is added:

The hands are cupped next to a candle while saying the following blessing:

בָּרוּךְ אַתָּה יהוה אֱלֹהֵינוּ מֶלֶךְ הָעוֹלָם, בּוֹרֵא מְאוֹרֵי הָאֵשׁ:

בָּרוּךְ אַתָּה יהוה אֱלֹהֵינוּ מֶלֶךְ הָעוֹלָם, הַמַּבְדִּיל בֵּין קֹדֶשׁ לְחוֹל, בֵּין אוֹר לְחוֹשֶׁךְ, בֵּין יִשְׂרָאֵל לָעַמִּים, בֵּין יוֹם הַשְּׁבִיעִי לְשֵׁשֶׁת יְמֵי הַמַּעֲשֶׂה, בֵּין קְדוּשַׁת שַׁבָּת לִקְדוּשַׁת יוֹם טוֹב הִבְדַּלְתָּ, וְאֶת יוֹם הַשְּׁבִיעִי מִשֵּׁשֶׁת יְמֵי הַמַּעֲשֶׂה קִדַּשְׁתָּ, הִבְדַּלְתָּ וְקִדַּשְׁתָּ אֶת עַמְּךָ יִשְׂרָאֵל בִּקְדוּשָׁתֶךָ: בָּרוּךְ אַתָּה יהוה הַמַּבְדִּיל בֵּין קֹדֶשׁ לְקֹדֶשׁ:

בָּרוּךְ אַתָּה יהוה אֱלֹהֵינוּ מֶלֶךְ הָעוֹלָם, שֶׁהֶחֱיָנוּ וְקִיְּמָנוּ וְהִגִּיעָנוּ לַזְּמַן הַזֶּה:

The entire cup of wine (or at least a majority of it) is now drunk. Men should recline on the left side while drinking the wine.

cups of wine correspond to the four decrees of Pharaoh against *Bnei Yisrael*: 1) slavery; 2) to kill all boys at birth; 3) to throw the boys into the river; 4) not to provide the slaves with straw to make the bricks. According to this opinion, women (who were not targeted with decrees number two or three) should only be obligated to drink two cups (*Shu"t Nishmas Chaim* 49). Obviously, this is not the halachah (*Shulchan Aruch* 472:14 clearly obligates women to drink the four cups of wine). It could also be argued that women were also affected by the decrees to kill the Jewish boys (who were their sons or brothers), so they would also have to drink the four cups (*S'dei Chemed, Chametz U'Matzah* 15:1).

There is a *minhag* that each person pours the wine for someone else at the Seder (*Rama* 473:1). Who, perhaps, should not pour for you?

According to the *Aruch HaShulchan* (473:6), one should not have his

On Saturday night, the following section is added:

> *The hands are cupped next to a candle while saying the following blessing:*
>
> *Blessed are You, Hashem, our God, King of the universe,*
> *Who creates the radiances of fire.*
>
> *Blessed are You, Hashem, our God, King of the universe, who distinguishes between the sacred and the profane, between light and darkness, between Israel and the nations, and between the seventh day and the six workdays. You distinguished between the holiness of the Sabbath and the holiness of the festivals, and You have sanctified the seventh day above the six workdays. You have distinguished and sanctified Your People Israel through Your holiness. Blessed are You, Hashem, who distinguishes between [one level of] holiness and [another level of] holiness.*

Blessed are You, Hashem, our God, King of the universe, who has granted us life, sustained us, and allowed us to reach this occasion.

The entire cup of wine (or at least a majority of it) is now drunk. Recline on the left side while drinking the wine.

wife pour for him, as it is considered דֶּרֶךְ גַּאֲוָה, arrogant, to command his wife to do so. Also, one should not have a child pour for him, since the child might come to break a cup or spill the wine (*Chaim L'Rosh, Beis HaKosos* 9). Both of these opinions are not brought in the *Mishnah Berurah* (see *Mishnah Berurah* 473:9).

Since reciting the Haggadah is a Torah obligation (rather than a Rabbinic mitzvah), we therefore do not say…

We do not say the *berachah* שֶׁעָשָׂה נִיסִּים on Seder night since we only make this *berachah* on Rabbinic mitzvos (*Maharil, Hilchos Haggadah*).

וּרְחַץ

The hands are washed with a cup of water. No blessing is recited.

כרפס

A small piece of vegetable (commonly used are celery and potatoes) is dipped in salt water or vinegar, and the following blessing is recited: While reciting this blessing one should bear in mind that it also covers the maror, which will be eaten later at the Seder.

בָּרוּךְ אַתָּה יהוה אֱלֹהֵינוּ מֶלֶךְ הָעוֹלָם, בּוֹרֵא פְּרִי הָאֲדָמָה:

The vegetable is eaten, without reclining.

How do we justify washing our hands at וּרְחַץ, but not washing our hands the entire year before eating other wet fruits or vegetables?

Some say that דָבָר שֶׁטִיבּוּלוֹ בְּמַשְׁקֶה (the requirement to wash one's hands before eating wet fruits or vegetables) is only applicable when you are actually eating דֶרֶךְ טִיבּוּל, with proper dipping, and not when the fruits are just wet (*Rav Dovid Aramah* on *Rambam, Berachos* 6:1). [For the practical halachah on washing hands prior to eating wet fruits or vegetables, see *Mishnah Berurah* 155:20.]

Some say to recline for *karpas*, while others say not to. How can one satisfy both opinions?

Since there is a *machlokes* whether or not one should recline for *karpas* (the *Birkei Yosef* 473:14 says not to recline, while the *Kitzur Shulchan Aruch* 119:3 says one should recline), there is an option given whereby one can satisfy both opinions. One can take two small pieces of *karpas*, dip both in salt water at the same time, and then eat one without reclining and one

URCHATZ

The hands are washed with a cup of water. No blessing is recited.

KARPAS

A small piece of vegetable (commonly used are celery and potatoes) is dipped in salt water, and the following blessing is recited: While reciting this blessing one should bear in mind that it also covers the maror, which will be eaten later at the Seder.

Blessed are You, Hashem, our God, King of the universe, who creates the produce of the ground.

The vegetable is eaten, without reclining.

while reclining (Rav Chaim Palagi in *Haggadas Chaim L'Rosh*, p. 89). This is not the common custom and is not brought in the *Mishnah Berurah*.

Who might not have to eat *karpas* at the Seder?

The *Beis Yosef* (*Tur* 483) explains that, according to the *Rif*, one who does not have wine and therefore makes Kiddush on matzos does not need to eat *karpas*, since *karpas* is the dipping of the vegetable **before** the meal starts. If one ate matzah for Kiddush, the meal has already begun, and it is too late to eat *karpas*! Once the meal has started, the children will not be stimulated to ask when they see the dipping of the *karpas* within the meal. (The halachah, however, is that one is required to eat *karpas* even in such a circumstance (see *Shulchan Aruch* 483:1) and the children are stimulated to ask by virtue of the fact that we dip twice [*karpas* and *maror*] even though both times are within the meal).

What is the connection between the *berachah* of *Ahavah Rabbah* and eating *karpas*?

The Chasam Sofer brings down from Rav Nosson Adler that *karpas* is

יחץ

The middle matzah is broken into two pieces, in such a manner that one piece is larger than the other. The larger piece is set aside to be eaten later as the "afikoman." The smaller half is placed back between the other two, and the Haggadah is recited over it.

what we call אפְי"א in most languages and צֶעלִיר (celery) in German. The Chasam Sofer says that the *roshei teivos*, first letters, of the words אֵ-ל פּוֹעֵל יְשׁוּעוֹת אַתָּה that we say in *Ahavah Rabbah* spell out אַפְי"א (*Shu"t Chasam Sofer, Orach Chaim* 132).

What kind of vegetable should not be used for *karpas*?

1. One should not use any vegetable that could be used for *maror*. According to the *Chochmas Shlomo* (473:5), one may use radish for *maror*. Therefore, one should not use it for *karpas*, as *karpas* should preferably be a kind of vegetable that cannot be used to fulfill the mitzvah of *maror*. See, however, *Kitzur Shulchan Aruch* (118:2), who states that it is preferable to use radish for *karpas* since, in his opinion, one cannot eat radish for *maror*.

2. One should not use a vegetable that will result in a bad breath. The Maharil would not use garlic or onion for *karpas* due to the resulting bad breath (*Eliyah Rabbah* 473:27), since one should have clean breath to relate the story of *Yetzias Mitzrayim*.

3. The *berachah* of הָאֲדָמָה on *karpas* is meant to exempt the *maror* from the *berachah* of הָאֲדָמָה. Therefore, one cannot use a vegetable that is usually eaten only cooked, which requires a שֶׁהַכֹּל when eaten raw [i.e., raw pumpkin; see *V'zos HaBerachah*, p. 191].

YACHATZ

The middle matzah is broken into two pieces, in such a manner that one piece is larger than the other. The larger piece is set aside to be eaten later as the "afikoman." The smaller half is placed back between the other two, and the Haggadah is recited over it.

What do we eat at the Seder that removes any last remnant of chametz from inside our stomachs?

Eating an appetizer before a meal causes an increase in appetite since it helps remove previous foods from the stomach. Likewise, the function of the *karpas* is to remove any last trace of chametz in our system, which prepares us to have an appetite for the matzah (*Shem Mi'Shmuel, Haggadah*).

Into which seven liquids may one dip *karpas*?

1. Vinegar (*Smag* 41)
2. Wine (ibid.)
3. *Charoses* (*Rambam* 8:2, *Chametz U'Matzah*)
4. A bit of *charoses* mixed with vinegar (*Darchei Moshe He'Aruch* 473).
5. Lemon juice (*Orchos Yosher*)
6. Salt (*Ohr Zarua* 256)
7. Salt water (*Tosefos Pesachim* 114a). Obviously, this is the common custom.

There are some authorities who do not require any dipping at all for *karpas* (see *Haggadah Sheleimah*, p. 103); this is not accepted by the *Shulchan Aruch* (473:6).

In what way does יַחַץ serve as a halachic reminder?

We break the middle matzah into two in order to remember not to take too long to recite the Haggadah, so that we will manage to eat the *afikoman* before midnight (*Olelos Yehudah*).

מַגִּיד

Throughout the Maggid section the matzah should be uncovered, in plain view, in fulfill-ment of the description of matzah as "bread over which much discussion [of the Exodus] is held" (Pesachim 36a).

The plate with the matzos is raised as the following paragraph is said:

הָא לַחְמָא עַנְיָא דִּי אֲכָלוּ אַבְהָתַנָא בְּאַרְעָא דְמִצְרָיִם. כָּל דִּכְפִין יֵיתֵי וְיֵכֻל. כָּל דִּצְרִיךְ יֵיתֵי וְיִפְסַח. הָשַׁתָּא הָכָא, לְשָׁנָה הַבָּאָה בְּאַרְעָא דְיִשְׂרָאֵל. הָשַׁתָּא עַבְדֵּי, לְשָׁנָה הַבָּאָה בְּנֵי חוֹרִין:

In which country would you find yourself doing "kapparos" on Seder night?

The *minhag* in Tunisia was to circle the קְעָרָה over the heads of the par-ticipants at the Seder in order to make the children ask; they would view this as a *segulah*, good omen, for success (*Chida, Ma'agal Tov*, p. 26).

How does הָא לַחְמָא עַנְיָא help us get along well with our non-Jewish neighbors?

הָא לַחְמָא עַנְיָא was written in Aramaic so that the non-Jews of that time could hear the Jewish people thank and praise Hashem for all He did for them. They would understand that the Jewish people are not ungrateful, and would reason that the Jews would surely also remember the kindness-es the non-Jews do for them as well. This ensured a pleasant relationship between the Jews and their non-Jewish neighbors (*Haggadas Ezor Eliyahu*).

What do we say in the Haggadah that was originally said only on erev Pesach?

כָּל דִּצְרִיךְ יֵיתֵי וְיִפְסַח, *anyone who needs can come and join our Pesach [of-fering]*, was usually said on *erev Pesach* before the *Korban Pesach* was

MAGGID

*Throughout the Maggid section the matzah should be uncovered, in plain view, in fulfill-
ment of the description of matzah as "bread over which much discussion [of the Exodus] is
held" (Pesachim 36a).*

The plate with the matzos is raised as the following paragraph is said:

THIS is the bread of affliction that our fathers ate in the land
of Egypt. Whoever is hungry, let him come and eat; whoever is
in need, let him come and celebrate Pesach. This year [we are]
here, next year in the land of Israel! This year [we are] slaves,
next year free men!

slaughtered, as one could only eat from the *Korban Pesach* if he was
numbered as part of the group before the *shechitah*. It was instituted
into the Haggadah text as a way to remember what was usually said
on the fourteenth of Nissan during the times of the Beis HaMikdash
(*Shibolei HaLeket*).

There are eleven things we do at the Seder to make the children ask. What are they?

1. We give out kernels and nuts to the children (*Shulchan Aruch*
   472:16).

2. We grab matzos from each other (חוֹטְפִין מַצָּה) so the children
   should see and ask. Some say that this is a source for the custom to "steal" the *afikoman*. (*Rambam, Chametz U'Matzah* 7:3).

3. We dip the *karpas* to make the children ask why we're eating
   vegetables before the meal, which is unusual (*Rashi, Pesachim*
   114a), or why we're dipping twice, *karpas* and *maror*, which is
   unusual (*Tosefos*, ibid.).

4. We give the children the four cups of wine (see *Mishnah
   Berurah* 472:46 and *Kaf HaChaim* 472:93).

מַה נִּשְׁתַּנָּה הַלַּיְלָה הַזֶּה מִכָּל הַלֵּילוֹת:

שֶׁבְּכָל הַלֵּילוֹת אָנוּ אוֹכְלִין חָמֵץ וּמַצָּה, הַלַּיְלָה הַזֶּה כֻּלּוֹ מַצָּה:

שֶׁבְּכָל הַלֵּילוֹת אָנוּ אוֹכְלִין שְׁאָר יְרָקוֹת, הַלַּיְלָה הַזֶּה מָרוֹר:

5. We lift the קְעָרָה while we recite הָא לַחְמָא עַנְיָא (*Shibolei HaLeket* 218).

6. We move the קְעָרָה to the end of the table before מַה נִּשְׁתַּנָּה (*Shulchan Aruch* 473:6). When a child asks why we do this, the answer is because we are not allowed to eat the meal before we speak about *Yetzias Mitzrayim*. Since the קְעָרָה has the matzos and the *maror* on it, by placing it at the end of the table, we are implying that we can't eat it just yet (*Mishnah Berurah* 473:66).

7. Pouring the second cup encourages the children to ask why we pour another cup before the meal has even begun (*Rashi, Pesachim* 116a).

8. We break the middle matzah into two pieces—יַחַץ (*Beis Yosef,* quoting *Orchos Chaim* 473).

9. We divide *Hallel* into two parts; we say half before the meal and half afterward (*Seder HaYom*).

10. We pour wine for each other but not for ourselves (as the Mishnah says in *Pesachim* 114a מָזְגוּ לוֹ, *they poured for him*), which is a significant deviation from the normal way of

The plate with the matzos is temporarily removed to the far end of the table.

The second cup of wine is poured, after which a child asks the following four questions.

WHY *is this night different from all other nights?*

FOR *on all nights we eat chametz and matzah, and on this night only matzah!*

FOR *on all nights we eat other vegetables, and on this night bitter herbs!*

pouring drinks, and is done to encourage the children to ask (*Seder Ha'Aruch*, p. 328).

11. The father wears a *kittel* (*Seder Ha'Aruch*, p. 75).

Rav Yosef Dov Soloveitchik (the *Beis HaLevi*) and his son Rav Chaim would not suffice with the prescribed number of rituals to advance the curiosity of the children. They would do many other unusual things at the Seder to encourage the children around the table to ask (ibid.).

When did מַה נִּשְׁתַּנָּה not include a question about reclining?

The Mishnah in *Pesachim* (116a) lists the questions of מַה נִּשְׁתַּנָּה, and in that Mishnah no question about reclining is recorded. Apparently, in those days it was quite normal to recline, so it did not warrant a question. In our text of the מַה נִּשְׁתַּנָּה we do ask about reclining, since for us it is an uncommon practice. This would seem to indicate that even today we need to recline, unlike the opinion of the *Ra'aviyah* (brought in *Tur* 472), who says that today there is no longer a need to recline since it is not considered a normal way to eat (*Aruch HaShulchan* 472:3).

The taste of the vegetable for *karpas* is bitter like maror. How so?

שֶׁבְּכָל הַלֵּילוֹת אָנוּ אוֹכְלִין שְׁאָר יְרָקוֹת הַלַּיְלָה הַזֶּה מָרוֹר, *on all other nights we eat all types of vegetables; on this night we eat maror.* This seems to imply that the only vegetable eaten on Seder night is the *maror*, but don't

שֶׁבְּכָל הַלֵּילוֹת אֵין אָנוּ מַטְבִּילִין אֲפִילוּ פַּעַם אֶחָת,
הַלַּיְלָה הַזֶּה שְׁתֵּי פְעָמִים:
שֶׁבְּכָל הַלֵּילוֹת אָנוּ אוֹכְלִין בֵּין יוֹשְׁבִין וּבֵין מְסוּבִּין,
הַלַּיְלָה הַזֶּה כֻּלָּנוּ מְסוּבִּין:

The plate with the matzos is returned to the table and the matzos are uncovered.

עֲבָדִים הָיִינוּ לְפַרְעֹה בְּמִצְרָיִם, וַיּוֹצִיאֵנוּ יהוה אֱלֹהֵינוּ
מִשָּׁם בְּיָד חֲזָקָה וּבִזְרוֹעַ נְטוּיָה. וְאִילּוּ לֹא הוֹצִיא הַקָּדוֹשׁ
בָּרוּךְ הוּא אֶת אֲבוֹתֵינוּ מִמִּצְרָיִם, הֲרֵי אָנוּ וּבָנֵינוּ וּבְנֵי

we eat a vegetable for *karpas* that is not bitter? The answer is that on this night, even the vegetable eaten for *karpas* tastes as bitter as the *maror*, since it reminds us of the slavery in Mitzrayim. Therefore, it is correct to say הַלַּיְלָה הַזֶּה מָרוֹר, *on this night we eat maror*, as the *karpas* vegetable also has bitter properties (*Peirush HaMeyuchas l'Rashi*).

Which other yom tov also engages children to ask a question that leads to talking about *Yetzias Mitzrayim*?

Sukkos. When children see that people move out of their homes and into a sukkah, they ask their parents about it. This leads their parents to elaborate on the story of *Yetzias Mitzrayim*—how Hashem took us out of Egypt and protected us in the wilderness. (*Rabbeinu Chananel* to *Sukkah* 2a, based on his explanation of *Vayikra* 23:43: "*In order that your generations should know,*" that is written in connection with the mitzvah of Sukkah).

Where do we find the halachic principles of שְׁתִיָּה בִּכְלַל אֲכִילָה, drinking is included in eating, and רוּבּוֹ כְּכוּלוֹ, the majority is like the whole, in the Haggadah?

We say שֶׁבְּכָל הַלֵּילוֹת אָנוּ אוֹכְלִין בֵּין יוֹשְׁבִין וּבֵין מְסוּבִּין, *on all other nights we **eat** sitting or reclining*, but on the night of Pesach we are all reclining.

FOR *on all nights we do not dip our food even once, and on this night we do it twice!*

FOR *on all nights we eat either sitting upright or reclining, and on this night we all recline!*

The plate with the matzos is returned to the table and the matzos are uncovered.

WE *were slaves to Pharaoh in Egypt, and Hashem, our God, took us out from there with a strong hand and with an out-stretched arm. And if the Holy One, Blessed is He, had not taken our ancestors out of Egypt, then we, our children, and*

Why don't we ask about the drinking of the four cups in a reclining manner just like we ask about eating while reclining? It must be because drinking is included in eating—שְׁתִיָּה בִּכְלַל אֲכִילָה (*Otzros HaHaggadah*, p. 454).

הַלַּיְלָה הַזֶּה כֻּלָּנוּ מְסֻבִּין, *on this night we are **all** reclining*. Even though a *talmid* before his *rebbi* does not need to recline, we can still say that we all recline since majority is like all—רוּבּוֹ כְּכוּלּוֹ (*Vehigadeta L'Vincha*, p. 22).

(Later in the Haggadah we find that the *Tanna'im* were מְסַפְּרִים בִּיצִיאַת מִצְרַיִם כָּל אוֹתוֹ הַלַּיְלָה, *talking about Yetzias Mitzrayim the entire night.* In order that we shouldn't think that it was רוּבּוֹ כְּכוּלּוֹ, that they only talked for the majority of the night, the Haggadah therefore adds that the *talmidim* came to tell them that it was time for *Kri'as Shema*, meaning that the *Tanna'im* really talked about *Yetzias Mitzrayim* the **entire** night (*Vayaged Shmuel*).

What should one tell his child before he starts עֲבָדִים הָיִינוּ?

It is not enough to simply say עֲבָדִים הָיִינוּ, *we were slaves,* etc., in order to answer the מַה נִּשְׁתַּנָּה, rather, each of the four questions must actually be answered separately. Why do we eat matzah? Since the dough of our ancestors did not have time to rise. Why do we eat *maror*?

בָּנֵינוּ מְשֻׁעְבָּדִים הָיִינוּ לְפַרְעֹה בְּמִצְרָיִם: וַאֲפִילוּ כֻּלָּנוּ
חֲכָמִים, כֻּלָּנוּ נְבוֹנִים, כֻּלָּנוּ זְקֵנִים, כֻּלָּנוּ יוֹדְעִים אֶת
הַתּוֹרָה, מִצְוָה עָלֵינוּ לְסַפֵּר בִּיצִיאַת מִצְרָיִם. וְכָל
הַמַּרְבֶּה לְסַפֵּר בִּיצִיאַת מִצְרַיִם, הֲרֵי זֶה מְשׁוּבָּח:
מַעֲשֶׂה בְּרַבִּי אֱלִיעֶזֶר וְרַבִּי יְהוֹשֻׁעַ וְרַבִּי אֶלְעָזָר בֶּן
עֲזַרְיָה וְרַבִּי עֲקִיבָא וְרַבִּי טַרְפוֹן שֶׁהָיוּ מְסוּבִּין בִּבְנֵי
בְרַק, וְהָיוּ מְסַפְּרִים בִּיצִיאַת מִצְרַיִם כָּל אוֹתוֹ הַלַּיְלָה,
עַד שֶׁבָּאוּ תַלְמִידֵיהֶם וְאָמְרוּ לָהֶם, רַבּוֹתֵינוּ הִגִּיעַ זְמַן
קְרִיאַת שְׁמַע שֶׁל שַׁחֲרִית:

Since the Egyptians embittered the lives of *Bnei Yisrael*. Why do we
recline? Since it is דֶּרֶךְ חֵירוּת, *the way of free people,* and tonight we are
demonstrating that freedom. Why do we dip twice? *Chazal* give two
answers: either to show דֶּרֶךְ חֵירוּת as well, as it is not the custom of
slaves to have appetizers, or it is meant to make the children ask that
very question, so that we can start talking about *Yetzias Mitzrayim*
(*Haggadas Rav Shlomo Zalman Auerbach*).

Why is no *berachah* recited before telling the story of the Exodus?

Since, had we merited, we would be telling over the story of our
redemption from this *galus* as well, and not just from Mitzrayim
(see *Yirmiyahu* 23:7). Therefore, if we see that the final redemption
has not yet arrived, we are reminded of the negative aspect of still
being in *galus*, and, as a result, we do not make a *berachah* (*Chesed
L'Avraham* 2:54).

The Rashba (*Shu"t* 1:18) writes that we don't make a *berachah* before

our children's children would still be subservient to Pharaoh in Egypt. Even if we were all wise, or we were all full of understanding, or we were all elders, or we were all knowledgeable in the Torah, it would still be incumbent upon us to recount the story of the Exodus from Egypt—and whoever expands upon the recounting of the story of the Exodus from Egypt is praiseworthy.

AN *incident happened with Rabbi Eliezer, Rabbi Yehoshua, Rabbi Elazar ben Azaryah, Rabbi Akiva and Rabbi Tarfon. They were reclining at the [Seder] table in Bnei Brak, and they were recounting the story of Exodus from Egypt all that night, until their students came in and told them: "Our Rabbis! The time for reciting the morning Shema has arrived!"*

giving tzedakah since the poor person might not accept it. Likewise, the mitzvah to *tell over the story of Yetzias Mitzrayim* (when one has children sitting around him) depends on the children listening—וּלְמַעַן תְּסַפֵּר בְּאָזְנֵי בִנְךָ, *and you should tell it in the ears of your children (Shemos 10:2)*—and they might not want to listen. Therefore, we don't make a *berachah (Machaneh Chaim 3:28).*

When might people pretend that midnight has already passed?

Rav Elazar ben Azaryah is of the opinion that the mitzvah of recounting *Yetzias Mitzrayim* only applies until midnight (*Mechilta, Bo* 18). If so, why did he talk about *Yetzias Mitzrayim* the whole night? The answer is that he was so involved in saying the story that he did not realize that midnight had passed.

On the other hand, there are people who have the opposite tendency of Rav Elazar ben Azaryah, and they are looking for ways to shorten telling over the story of the Exodus. The author of the Haggadah feared that if the text mentioned that *sippur Yetzias Mitzrayim* only

אָמַר רַבִּי אֶלְעָזָר בֶּן עֲזַרְיָה הֲרֵי אֲנִי כְּבֶן שִׁבְעִים שָׁנָה, וְלֹא זָכִיתִי שֶׁתֵּאָמֵר יְצִיאַת מִצְרַיִם בַּלֵּילוֹת עַד שֶׁדְּרָשָׁהּ בֶּן זוֹמָא, שֶׁנֶּאֱמַר לְמַעַן תִּזְכֹּר אֶת יוֹם צֵאתְךָ מֵאֶרֶץ מִצְרַיִם כֹּל יְמֵי חַיֶּיךָ. יְמֵי חַיֶּיךָ הַיָּמִים, כֹּל יְמֵי חַיֶּיךָ הַלֵּילוֹת. וַחֲכָמִים אוֹמְרִים יְמֵי חַיֶּיךָ הָעוֹלָם הַזֶּה, כֹּל יְמֵי חַיֶּיךָ לְהָבִיא לִימוֹת הַמָּשִׁיחַ:

is applicable until midnight (according to Rav Elazar ben Azaryah's opinion), people would take advantage to get out of doing the mitzvah. Some dishonest people could act as if midnight had already passed so they would no longer be obligated in the mitzvah. In order to avoid this, the author of the Haggadah preferred not to write this obligation openly (*Rav Yehudah ben Rav Yakar*).

How old was Rav Elazar ben Azaryah when he said,
"הֲרֵי אֲנִי כְּבֶן שִׁבְעִים שָׁנָה"—*I am like a seventy-year-old person?*

There are different opinions as to how old he really was at the time:

- Twelve (*Sefer Ha'orah*)
- Thirteen (*Abudraham*, quoting the *Yerushalmi*)
- Sixteen (*Yerushalmi Berachos* 4:1)
- Seventeen (*Rav Nissim Gaon, Berachos* 27b)
- Eighteen (*Rashi, Berachos* 12b)
- Fifty (*Maharal, Gevuros Hashem*, ch. 53)
- Sixty-eight or sixty-nine (*Charedim* to *Yerushalmi Berachos* 1:6)
- Seventy (*Tosefos Ri Shirla'on* to *Berachos* 28a, quoted in *Otzros HaHaggadah*, p. 476)

RABBI *Elazar ben Azaryah said: I am like a seventy-year-old man, yet I did not merit [to demonstrate why] the Exodus from Egypt should be mentioned every night, until Ben Zoma explained it: It says (Devarim 16:3), "So that you remember the day you left Egypt all the days of your life." Just "the days of your life" would have referred to the days; "all the days of your life" therefore refers to the nights as well. But the other sages say that just "the days of your life" would have referred to the present world; the addition of the word "all" comes to include the Messianic era as well.*

Who "tipped the scales"?

There was a dispute between Rav Elazar ben Azaryah and the *Chachamim* regarding whether one has to mention *Yetzias Mitzrayim* at night. Half of the *talmidei chachamim* ruled one way, and half ruled the other way. The matter was therefore undecided. Then Ben Zoma came along and tipped the scales in favor of Rav Elazar ben Azaryah (*Haggadah Zero'a Netuyah*).

בָּרוּךְ הַמָּקוֹם—In what way can the gematria of Hashem's four-letter name equal מָקוֹם?

If you multiply each letter of Hashem's four-letter name by itself (i.e., י equals 10, and 10 x 10 = 100, and so forth) and add all the numbers together, you get 186, which is the gematria of מָקוֹם (*Abudraham*). Another way is to take the first two letters of Hashem's name and multiply their numerical value by each other twice (י is 10 and ה is 5, 10 x 5 = 50 and 5 x 10 = 50) and then do the same with the last two letters (ו is 6 and ה is 5, 6 x 5 = 30 and 5 x 6 = 30) which equals 160. If you add the gematria of Hashem's name (26) to that total, you also end up with 186, the gematria of מָקוֹם (*Sefer HaKaneh*).

בָּרוּךְ הַמָּקוֹם, בָּרוּךְ הוּא. בָּרוּךְ שֶׁנָּתַן תּוֹרָה לְעַמּוֹ
יִשְׂרָאֵל, בָּרוּךְ הוּא:

כְּנֶגֶד אַרְבָּעָה בָנִים דִּבְּרָה תּוֹרָה: אֶחָד חָכָם, וְאֶחָד
רָשָׁע, וְאֶחָד תָּם, וְאֶחָד שֶׁאֵינוֹ יוֹדֵעַ לִשְׁאוֹל:

חָכָם מָה הוּא אוֹמֵר: מָה הָעֵדֹת וְהַחֻקִּים וְהַמִּשְׁפָּטִים
אֲשֶׁר צִוָּה יְהֹוָה אֱלֹהֵינוּ אֶתְכֶם. וְאַף אַתָּה אֱמָר לוֹ
כְּהִלְכוֹת הַפֶּסַח, אֵין מַפְטִירִין אַחַר הַפֶּסַח אֲפִיקוֹמָן:

רָשָׁע מָה הוּא אוֹמֵר: מָה הָעֲבֹדָה הַזֹּאת לָכֶם. לָכֶם
וְלֹא לוֹ. וּלְפִי שֶׁהוֹצִיא אֶת עַצְמוֹ מִן הַכְּלָל כָּפַר בְּעִקָּר,
וְאַף אַתָּה הַקְהֵה אֶת שִׁנָּיו וֶאֱמָר לוֹ, בַּעֲבוּר זֶה עָשָׂה
יהוה לִי בְּצֵאתִי מִמִּצְרָיִם: לִי וְלֹא לוֹ. אִלּוּ הָיָה שָׁם לֹא
הָיָה נִגְאָל:

When does dessert come before the meal?

Since we can't eat anything (including dessert) after the *afikoman*, we eat dessert before the *seudah*. This is done by giving the children קְלָיוֹת וֶאֱגוֹזִים, kernels and nuts (or chocolates and candies) before the meal. This is the question of the wise son: *Why did we start the meal with dessert?* The answer is: We can't eat anything after the *afikoman*, so we ate the dessert first (*Kolbo* 51).

Which one short word did Rav Zalman Voloʒhiner add to the Haggadah in the answer to the חָכָם?

In the answer to the חָכָם, we say to him, כְּהִלְכוֹת הַפֶּסַח אֵין מַפְטִירִין אַחַר הַפֶּסַח אֲפִיקוֹמָן, *like the laws of Pesach—we do not eat after eating the*

BLESSED *be the Omnipresent! Blessed be He! Blessed be the One Who gave the Torah to His People Israel! Blessed be He!*

THE *Torah speaks of four different kinds of sons: One who is wise, one who is wicked, one who is simple, and one who does not know enough to ask questions.*

WHAT *does the wise son say? "What are the testimonies and the statutes and the laws that Hashem, our God, has commanded you?" (Devarim 6:20). You, in turn, should tell him all about the laws of the Pesach offering, [for instance]: "One may not eat any dessert after the meat of the Pesach offering."*

WHAT *does the wicked son say? "What is this service to you?" (Shemos 12:26)—implying "to you," but not "to him!" Because he excludes himself from the rest of the community he has denied a fundamental principle. You, in turn, should blunt his teeth and tell him: "Because of this Hashem did for me when I left Egypt" (ibid. 13:8)—implying "for me," but not "for him!" If he had been there then, he would not have been redeemed.*

afikoman, which sounds like we only tell him this halachah of not eating after the *afikoman*. Rav Zalman added one word כְּהִלְכוֹת הַפֶּסַח עַד אֵין מַפְטִירִין אַחַר הַפֶּסַח אֲפִיקוֹמָן, *like the laws of Pesach* **until** *[you get to the final halachah of] not eating after the afikoman*, implying that one has to teach the חָכָם everything about Pesach, until the very last halachah. The Brisker Rav used to say this piece of the Haggadah twice, first like the way it is printed, and the second time according to Rav Zalman's correction (*Haggadah Mi'Beis Levi*, p. 109).

Which minhag is no longer relevant today due to the fact that kids or adults have hidden the afikoman?

The *Shibolei HaLeket* (218) wrote that when a person says the

תָּם מָה הוּא אוֹמֵר: מַה זֹּאת. וְאָמַרְתָּ אֵלָיו בְּחֹזֶק יָד
הוֹצִיאָנוּ יְהֹוָה מִמִּצְרַיִם מִבֵּית עֲבָדִים:

וְשֶׁאֵינוֹ יוֹדֵעַ לִשְׁאוֹל אַתְּ פְּתַח לוֹ, שֶׁנֶּאֱמַר, וְהִגַּדְתָּ
לְבִנְךָ בַּיּוֹם הַהוּא לֵאמֹר בַּעֲבוּר זֶה עָשָׂה יְהֹוָה לִי
בְּצֵאתִי מִמִּצְרָיִם:

words, כְּהִלְכוֹת הַפֶּסַח אֵין מַפְטִירִין אַחַר הַפֶּסַח אֲפִיקוֹמָן, *like the laws of Pesach—we do not eat after eating the afikoman,* he should lift up the piece of matzah set aside for the *afikoman* to show it to all the participants at the Seder. In our days, when that piece of matzah has been hidden, this *minhag* is no longer practiced (*Vayaged Moshe* 22:4).

How did people like Dasan and Aviram deserve to be redeemed from Mitzrayim?

We tell the wicked son, "*If you had been there, you would not have been redeemed.*" Seemingly, Dasan and Aviram made their way out even though they were *resha'im*, so what message are we giving the wicked son? The answer is that Dasan and Aviram brought the *Korban Pesach* prior to leaving Mitzrayim, so they therefore were allowed to go out even though they were *resha'im*. But the wicked son, who ridicules bringing the *Korban Pesach* (מַה הָעֲבוֹדָה הַזֹּאת לָכֶם), wouldn't have brought it in Mitzrayim, and therefore would not have been allowed to leave (*Haggadas Birkas HaShir*).

Which son would ask his father, "Why are you giving this kohen money if he did not do you any favors or give you anything in return?"

This is the question of the *tam*, as it appears in the Torah itself. The

WHAT *does the simple son say? "What is this?" (ibid. 13:14). "And you shall say to him: With a strong hand Hashem took us out of Egypt, from the house of bondage" (ibid.).*

AS *for the one who does not know enough to ask questions—you must open for him, as it says, "You shall tell your child on that day: Because of this Hashem did for me when I left Egypt" (Shemos 13:8).*

question of מַה זֹאת, *what is this*, appears in the middle of the *pesukim* regarding *pidyon haben*. The son asks his father, "Why do you give the *kohen* money when he is not giving you anything in return?" Then the Torah obligates us to answer him with the story of *Yetzias Mitzrayim* and explain why the firstborn deserves to be redeemed (*Kli Yakar, Shemos* 13:14).

Who needs to be told from A to Z?

To the son who does not know how to ask, the Haggadah says אַתְּ פְּתַח לוֹ, *you should start telling him*. The word אַתְּ hints to the fact that this child should be taught the entire story from א to ת (*Divrei Chaim* quoted in *Otzros HaHaggadah*, p. 502).

Which word in Hebrew can mean both to speak harshly and softly?

The word וְהִגַּדְתָּ, *and you should tell*, can mean with harsh words (see *Rashi, Yisro* 19:3), or it can mean with soft words (see *Chagigah* 14a). Therefore, the phrase וְהִגַּדְתָּ לְבִנְךָ בַּיוֹם הַהוּא לֵאמֹר בַּעֲבוּר זֶה עָשָׂה ה' לִי בְּצֵאתִי מִמִּצְרָיִם, *and you should tell your son on that day saying, "It is because of this that Hashem did for me when I left Mitzrayim,"* is understood to be the answer for both the *rasha* (a harsh reply) as well as the answer to the one who does not know how to ask (a soft reply) (*Kli Yakar, Shemos* 12:26).

יָכוֹל מֵרֹאשׁ חוֹדֶשׁ, תַּלְמוּד לוֹמַר בַּיּוֹם הַהוּא. אִי
בַּיּוֹם הַהוּא יָכוֹל מִבְּעוֹד יוֹם, תַּלְמוּד לוֹמַר בַּעֲבוּר
זֶה. בַּעֲבוּר זֶה לֹא אָמַרְתִּי אֶלָּא בְּשָׁעָה שֶׁיֵּשׁ מַצָּה
וּמָרוֹר מוּנָּחִים לְפָנֶיךָ:

How long before Pesach must one start studying the relevant halachos?

There is a *machlokes* in the Gemara in *Pesachim* (6a) whether one has to start giving *derashos* about the halachos of the upcoming Yom Tov thirty days or two weeks before (according to the views of the *Chachamim* and Rabban Shimon ben Gamliel, respectively). The Haggadah says that one might have thought that he can fulfill the mitzvah of *sippur Yetzias Mitzrayim* from Rosh Chodesh. Why would someone think that? Because we're studying the laws of Pesach from then (from Rosh Chodesh)! Apparently, the Haggadah follows the opinion of Rabban Shimon ben Gamliel (*Sefer Ha'Orah* 90). (Nevertheless the practical halachah is in accordance with the *Chachamim, Shulchan Aruch* 429:1.)

Which of the four sons has the earliest bedtime?

The Haggadah says יָכוֹל מִבְּעוֹד יוֹם—one may think he can fulfill the mitzvah of *sippur Yetzias Mitzrayim* if he talks about *Yetzias Mitzrayim* while it is still day. Why? Because the child who does not know how to ask is a young boy who goes to sleep early. Therefore, we could think that you can start telling him about *Yetzias Mitzrayim* while it is still daytime on *erev Pesach*. Nevertheless, due to the requirement of having the matzah and *maror* in front of you when you relay the story, the mitzvah can't be done by day (*Otzros HaHaggadah*, p. 506).

ONE *might think (that the recounting of the Exodus to one's children) should be done from the first of the month. Therefore the Torah says, "On that day" (ibid.). But based on the words "On that day" one might think that it should be done while it is still daytime. Therefore the Torah says, "Because of this" (ibid.), implying that "I am speaking only of the time when matzah and maror are placed before you."*

If one misses reciting the Haggadah at night, can he make it up by saying it during the first day of yom tov?

The *Magen Avraham* (485:1) says that according to the opinion of the *Olas Shabbos*, if one did not recite the Haggadah at night, he can do so by day. The *Magen Avraham* himself argues that this is not correct, as there is a requirement to have the *matzah and maror placed in front of you* when you say the story, which means that you can only do the mitzvah of reciting the Haggadah at a time that is fit for the mitzvah of matzah and *maror* (at night).

The *Chok Yaakov* (473:1) says that the *Magen Avraham* misunderstood the *Olas Shabbos*, who was actually referring to making up the lost Kiddush from Seder night (just like one can make up the lost Friday night Kiddush on Shabbos day, *Shulchan Aruch* 271:8), but he was not referring to making up the actual Haggadah.

Who has finished the Haggadah when he says בְּשָׁעָה שֶׁיֵּשׁ מַצָּה וּמָרוֹר מֻנָּחִים לְפָנֶיךָ, at the time the matzah and maror are placed in front of you?

According to Shmuel (*Pesachim* 116a) one has to start the Haggadah with disgrace (גְּנוּת) and finish with praise (שֶׁבַח). The disgrace refers to *Avadim Hayinu*. The praise includes mention of *Pesach*, matzah, and *maror*. We already mentioned *Pesach* in the answer to the חָכָם

מִתְּחִלָּה עוֹבְדֵי עֲבוֹדָה זָרָה הָיוּ אֲבוֹתֵינוּ, וְעַכְשָׁיו קֵרְבָנוּ הַמָּקוֹם לַעֲבוֹדָתוֹ, שֶׁנֶּאֱמַר, וַיֹּאמֶר יְהוֹשֻׁעַ אֶל כָּל הָעָם כֹּה אָמַר יְהוָֹה אֱלֹהֵי יִשְׂרָאֵל בְּעֵבֶר הַנָּהָר יָשְׁבוּ אֲבוֹתֵיכֶם מֵעוֹלָם, תֶּרַח אֲבִי אַבְרָהָם וַאֲבִי נָחוֹר, וַיַּעַבְדוּ אֱלֹהִים אֲחֵרִים: וָאֶקַּח אֶת אֲבִיכֶם אֶת אַבְרָהָם מֵעֵבֶר הַנָּהָר, וָאוֹלֵךְ אוֹתוֹ בְּכָל אֶרֶץ כְּנָעַן, וָאַרְבֶּה אֶת זַרְעוֹ, וָאֶתֶּן לוֹ אֶת יִצְחָק: וָאֶתֵּן לְיִצְחָק אֶת יַעֲקֹב וְאֶת עֵשָׂו, וָאֶתֵּן לְעֵשָׂו אֶת הַר שֵׂעִיר לָרֶשֶׁת אוֹתוֹ, וְיַעֲקֹב וּבָנָיו יָרְדוּ מִצְרָיִם:

(כְּהִלְכוֹת הַפֶּסַח אֵין מַפְטִירִין אַחַר הַפֶּסַח אֲפִיקוֹמָן), and we also talked about matzah and *maror* to explain why the obligation to relate *Yetzias Mitzrayim* is only at night (בְּשָׁעָה שֶׁיֵּשׁ מַצָּה וּמָרוֹר מֻנָּחִים לְפָנֶיךָ). Shmuel would therefore say that the Haggadah is now finished (*Rav Yehudah ben Rav Yakar*). [Practically speaking, we also follow Rav's view that one has to start with מִתְּחִלָּה עוֹבְדֵי עֲבוֹדָה זָרָה הָיוּ אֲבוֹתֵינוּ, *at first our ancestors were idol worshippers,* and continue all the way through the rest of the Haggadah.]

What is done to be mekarev the wicked son at the Seder?

Chazal tell us that "the left hand should push away and the right hand should bring close" (*Sotah* 47a). We have pushed away the רָשָׁע with a sharp reply; now is the time to be *mekarev* him. We tell the רָשָׁע that there is still hope for him, as even our own ancestors were idol worshippers and managed to turn into people who serve Hashem (*Otzros HaHaggadah,* p. 508).

ORIGINALLY *our ancestors were idol worshippers, but now the Omnipresent has drawn us near to His service. Thus it says, "Yehoshua said to all the People: Thus said Hashem, the God of Israel: Your ancestors had always dwelt on the other side of the river—Terach, the father of Avraham and the father of Nachor—and they worshipped other gods. Then I took your father Avraham from the other side of the [Euphrates] River, and I had him travel throughout all of the land of Canaan. I increased his offspring and gave him Yitzchak, and to Yitzchak I gave Yaakov and Eisav. To Eisav I gave Mount Se'ir to take possession of, and Yaakov and his sons went down to Egypt"* (Yehoshua 24:2–4).

מִתְּחִלָּה עוֹבְדֵי עֲבוֹדָה זָרָה הָיוּ אֲבוֹתֵינוּ, **In the beginning, our forefathers served idols. Who does this refer to? Who served idols?**

According to the Rambam (*Hilchos Avodas Kochavim* 1:3) even Avraham Avinu was raised to serve עֲבוֹדָה זָרָה and did so until he discovered the existence of Hashem. He also writes that in Mitzrayim, the Jewish people, except for members of *shevet Levi*, started serving idols. However, the Ritva (commentary to the Haggadah) states that Avraham Avinu never served idols. Likewise, *Midrash Rabbeinu David HaNagid* holds that the Jewish people in Mitzrayim never served עֲבוֹדָה זָרָה. (This needs further clarification, as there are explicit references to idol worship in Mitzrayim; see *Yehoshua* 24:14 and *Yechezkel* 20:8 as well as *Chazal* in *Mechilta, Bo* 5 and other midrashim to that effect).

On the night of the Seder, one has to view himself as if he left Mitzrayim. What other concept requires one to imagine himself in a different light?

Just like one has to view himself as if he left Mitzrayim on Seder night, he also has to view himself as if he used to serve עֲבוֹדָה זָרָה and has just begun serving Hashem (*Chasam Sofer, Derashos* 2, p. 268).

בָּרוּךְ שׁוֹמֵר הַבְטָחָתוֹ לְיִשְׂרָאֵל, בָּרוּךְ הוּא.
שֶׁהַקָּדוֹשׁ בָּרוּךְ הוּא חִשַּׁב אֶת הַקֵּץ, לַעֲשׂוֹת כְּמָה
שֶׁאָמַר לְאַבְרָהָם אָבִינוּ בִּבְרִית בֵּין הַבְּתָרִים,
שֶׁנֶּאֱמַר, וַיֹּאמֶר לְאַבְרָם יָדֹעַ תֵּדַע כִּי גֵר יִהְיֶה זַרְעֲךָ
בְּאֶרֶץ לֹא לָהֶם וַעֲבָדוּם וְעִנּוּ אֹתָם אַרְבַּע מֵאוֹת
שָׁנָה: וְגַם אֶת הַגּוֹי אֲשֶׁר יַעֲבֹדוּ דָּן אָנֹכִי, וְאַחֲרֵי כֵן
יֵצְאוּ בִּרְכֻשׁ גָּדוֹל:

The matzah is covered and the cup of wine is raised while reciting the following paragraph:

וְהִיא שֶׁעָמְדָה לַאֲבוֹתֵינוּ וְלָנוּ, שֶׁלֹּא אֶחָד
בִּלְבָד עָמַד עָלֵינוּ לְכַלּוֹתֵינוּ, אֶלָּא שֶׁבְּכָל
דּוֹר וָדוֹר עוֹמְדִים עָלֵינוּ לְכַלּוֹתֵינוּ, וְהַקָּדוֹשׁ
בָּרוּךְ הוּא מַצִּילֵנוּ מִיָּדָם:

וָאֶתֵּן לְעֵשָׂו אֶת הַר שֵׂעִיר, *and I gave Har Se'ir*
to Eisav. What grew on Har Se'ir?

Many small pieces of reeds grew on *Har Se'ir* and gave the impression
that the mountain was "covered in reeds" just like a person's head is
covered in hair (the word שֵׂעִיר being related to the word שֵׂעָר, hair)
(*Aderes Eliyahu, Yehoshua* 15:10).

How does 210y + 6c = 400y?

The decree of servitude in Mitzrayim was for a period of four hundred
years (*Bereishis* 15:13), meaning, there was a decree that *Bnei Yisrael*
would have to complete a certain quota of slave labor that normally would take four hundred years to complete. However, due to the
population growth of the Jewish people (six children born from each

BLESSED *be the One Who keeps His promise to Israel! Blessed be He! For the Holy One, Blessed is He, calculated the end [of our captivity], in order to fulfill what He had said to our forefather Avraham at the Covenant Between the Parts, as it says, "And He said to Avraham: 'Know with certainty that your offspring will be strangers in a land not theirs, and [your off-spring] will serve them, and they will oppress [your offspring], for 400 years. And also the nation whom they will serve, I will judge, and afterwards they will leave with great possessions' "*
(*Bereishis* 15:13–14).

The matzah is covered and the cup of wine is raised while reciting the following paragraph:

AND it is this that has stood by our fathers and by us! For it is not just one individual who rose against us to annihilate us, but in every single generation people rise up against us to annihilate us, and the Holy One, Blessed is He, saves us from their hands!

pregnancy), they managed to complete the equivalent of four hundred years of slave labor in a shorter time, as they had more people to carry out the jobs (*Peroshas Derachim*, *derush* 5).

Where is there a source for calling your child a treasure?

"...And afterward they will leave with a **great treasure**" (*Bereishis* 15:14). The "great treasure" in this *pasuk* refers to the many children they had in Mitzrayim (*Otzros HaHaggadah*, p. 525).

Where in וְהִיא שֶׁעָמְדָה do we see why "they rise up against us to destroy us"?

The Sefas Emes explains that we can read שֶׁלֹּא אֶחָד בִּלְבָד עָמַד עָלֵינוּ לְכַלּוֹתֵינוּ as follows: Due to שֶׁלֹּא אֶחָד, *that we are not united as one*, בִּלְבָד,

The cup is put down and the matzah is uncovered.

צֵא וּלְמַד מַה בִּקֵּשׁ לָבָן הָאֲרַמִּי לַעֲשׂוֹת לְיַעֲקֹב אָבִינוּ, שֶׁפַּרְעֹה לֹא גָזַר אֶלָּא עַל הַזְּכָרִים, וְלָבָן בִּקֵּשׁ לַעֲקוֹר אֶת הַכֹּל, שֶׁנֶּאֱמַר, אֲרַמִּי אֹבֵד אָבִי וַיֵּרֶד מִצְרַיְמָה וַיָּגָר שָׁם בִּמְתֵי מְעָט, וַיְהִי שָׁם לְגוֹי גָּדוֹל עָצוּם וָרָב:

that in itself explains why עָמַד עָלֵינוּ לְכַלּוֹתֵינוּ, *they rise up against us to destroy us.* As we know, the cause of our current *galus* is due to שִׂנְאַת חִנָּם (baseless hatred), and we need to improve in that area to merit the ultimate *geulah.*

וְהַקָּדוֹשׁ בָּרוּךְ הוּא מַצִּילֵנוּ מִיָּדָם—Which present miracle is greater than all of the miracles of *Yetzias Mitzrayim*?

The miracle of the Jewish People's existence to this very day, with all the persecutions and exiles we had to go through, is a far greater miracle than all the miracles of *Yetzias Mitzrayim* (Ya'avetz, in the foreword to his siddur).

When would the text of אֲרַמִּי אֹבֵד אָבִי be said differently from how it is today?

The Torah mentions the *pesukim* recited by one who brings *bikkurim* (first fruits) to the Beis HaMikdash (*Devarim* 26:5-10). In our Haggadah, we expound upon the first four of these *pesukim* (26:5-8), which discuss the slavery and redemption from Mitzrayim. The next *pasuk* discusses coming to Eretz Yisrael—וַיְבִאֵנוּ אֶל הַמָּקוֹם הַזֶּה, *and He brought us to this place* (26:9)—while the following *pasuk* (26:10) discusses bringing the actual *bikkurim,* and as such both are not related to the Pesach Seder.

One who was in the Land of Israel during the times of the Beis HaMikdash would add וַיְבִאֵנוּ אֶל הַמָּקוֹם הַזֶּה, *and He brought us to this*

The cup is put down and the matzah is uncovered.

GO *out and learn what Lavan the Aramean wanted to do to our father Yaakov. For Pharaoh decreed only against the male children, but Lavan sought to obliterate everyone, as it says:* **"An Aramean [sought to] destroy my forefather. And he went down to Egypt and sojourned there with a small number of people, and there he became a great, powerful, and numerous nation"** *(Devarim 26:5).*

place... (Devarim 26:9) during his recitation of the Haggadah, but it is likely that this was not said in *Chutz La'aretz* even when the Beis HaMikdash was standing (*Shu"t Melamed Leho'il* 3:65).

אֲרַמִּי אֹבֵד אָבִי can mean "An Arami (Lavan) wanted to kill my father (Yaakov)." What else can it mean?

My father (Yaakov), who lived in Aram, was a pauper (אֹבֵד) (*Ibn Ezra, Devarim* 26:5); my father (Avraham), who was from Aram, went from place to place (אֹבֵד) to reach Eretz Yisrael (Rashbam, ibid.) An Arami (Besuel, father of Lavan) wanted to destroy my father (Yitzchak) by placing poison in the food of Eliezer the servant of Avraham, thereby preventing the marriage between Yitzchak and Rivkah (Yonasan ben Uziel); or, an Arami (Bilaam) advised Pharaoh to destroy my father (the Jewish people) (*Shelah, Seder Ha'Aruch*, p. 411).

Who caused the feelings of jealousy that the brothers felt toward Yosef, which eventually brought all of Yaakov's family down to Mitzrayim?

The character traits of hatred and jealousy that we find in the conflict between Yosef and his brothers were inherited from Lavan. Lavan was the maternal grandfather of all the *shevatim* (as even Bilhah and Zilpah were Lavan's offspring, *Pirkei D'Rebbi Eliezer* 36). Thus, Lavan's wicked *middos* eventually manifested themselves on

וַיֵּרֶד מִצְרַיְמָה, אָנוּס עַל פִּי הַדִּבּוּר:

וַיָּגָר שָׁם, מְלַמֵּד שֶׁלֹּא יָרַד יַעֲקֹב אָבִינוּ לְהִשְׁתַּקֵּעַ בְּמִצְרַיִם אֶלָּא לָגוּר שָׁם, שֶׁנֶּאֱמַר, וַיֹּאמְרוּ אֶל פַּרְעֹה לָגוּר בָּאָרֶץ בָּאנוּ, כִּי אֵין מִרְעֶה לַצֹּאן אֲשֶׁר לַעֲבָדֶיךָ, כִּי כָבֵד הָרָעָב בְּאֶרֶץ כְּנָעַן, וְעַתָּה יֵשְׁבוּ נָא עֲבָדֶיךָ בְּאֶרֶץ גֹּשֶׁן:

בִּמְתֵי מְעָט, כְּמָה שֶׁנֶּאֱמַר, בְּשִׁבְעִים נֶפֶשׁ יָרְדוּ אֲבֹתֶיךָ מִצְרָיְמָה, וְעַתָּה שָׂמְךָ יהוה אֱלֹהֶיךָ כְּכוֹכְבֵי הַשָּׁמַיִם לָרֹב:

וַיְהִי שָׁם לְגוֹי, מְלַמֵּד שֶׁהָיוּ יִשְׂרָאֵל מְצֻיָּנִים שָׁם:

גָּדוֹל עָצוּם, כְּמָה שֶׁנֶּאֱמַר, וּבְנֵי יִשְׂרָאֵל פָּרוּ וַיִּשְׁרְצוּ וַיִּרְבּוּ וַיַּעַצְמוּ בִּמְאֹד מְאֹד וַתִּמָּלֵא הָאָרֶץ אֹתָם:

a certain level in the *shevatim*. That is the connection between אֲרַמִּי אֹבֵד אָבִי וַיֵּרֶד מִצְרָיְמָה, *an Arami (Lavan) wanted to kill my father (Yaakov), and he went down to Mitzrayim.* Due to the influence of Lavan (who caused Yaakov's children to feel jealousy toward Yosef), Yaakov and his children had to go down to Mitzrayim (*Abarbanel, Devarim* 26:5).

The *Mahari Bei Rav* (quoted in *Otzros HaHaggadah*, p. 533) gives another reason. Had Lavan not switched around Rachel and Leah, then Yosef would have been born first, and, as the *bechor*, he would not have experienced the brothers' jealousy. (Apparently, Rachel would have been able to have children right away if she had married Yaakov before Leah did.) But since Lavan switched the order, Yosef was born

AND *he went down to Egypt*—compelled by Divine decree.

AND sojourned there—*This teaches that our father Yaakov did not go down to settle in Egypt permanently, but to (temporarily) sojourn there. Thus it says, "[Yaakov's sons] said to Pharaoh: 'We have come to sojourn in the land, for there is no pasture for your servants' sheep, because the famine is severe in the land of Canaan. So now, let your servants please dwell in the land of Goshen'" (Bereishis 47:4).*

WITH a small number of people—*as it says: "With seventy souls your forefathers went down to Egypt, and now Hashem your God has made you as numerous as the stars of heaven" (Devarim 10:22).*

AND there he became a ... nation—*this teaches that the Israelites were distinctive there.*

GREAT, powerful—*as it says: "And the Children of Israel were fruitful and proliferated and became very, very powerful, and the land became filled with them" (Shemos 1:7).*

last. Since he was not the *bechor*, the special manner in which he was treated caused jealousy, which eventually led the family down to Mitzrayim.

Which part of Mitzrayim borders on Eretz Yisrael?

Goshen. So as to not assimilate into the Egyptian culture, the *shevatim* decided to settle on the outskirts of Mitzrayim in Goshen, a place that borders on Eretz Yisrael (*Ba'alei Tosefos Bereishis* 46:29).

What do Serach bas Asher and Chushim ben Dan have in common (besides both being grandchildren of Yaakov Avinu)?

In *Parashas Vayigash* the Torah lists seventy people as going down to Mitzrayim with Yaakov (46:27), but only sixty-nine people are

וָרֵב, כְּמָה שֶׁנֶּאֱמַר, רְבָבָה כְּצֶמַח הַשָּׂדֶה נְתַתִּיךְ, וַתִּרְבִּי וַתִּגְדְּלִי וַתָּבֹאִי בַּעֲדִי עֲדָיִים, שָׁדַיִם נָכֹנוּ וּשְׂעָרֵךְ צִמֵּחַ וְאַתְּ עֵרֹם וְעֶרְיָה: וָאֶעֱבֹר עָלַיִךְ וָאֶרְאֵךְ מִתְבּוֹסֶסֶת בְּדָמָיִךְ, וָאֹמַר לָךְ בְּדָמַיִךְ חֲיִי, וָאֹמַר לָךְ בְּדָמַיִךְ חֲיִי:

וַיָּרֵעוּ אֹתָנוּ הַמִּצְרִים וַיְעַנּוּנוּ, וַיִּתְּנוּ עָלֵינוּ עֲבֹדָה קָשָׁה:

וַיָּרֵעוּ אֹתָנוּ הַמִּצְרִים, כְּמָה שֶׁנֶּאֱמַר, הָבָה נִתְחַכְּמָה לוֹ פֶּן יִרְבֶּה וְהָיָה כִּי תִקְרֶאנָה מִלְחָמָה וְנוֹסַף גַּם הוּא עַל שֹׂנְאֵינוּ וְנִלְחַם בָּנוּ וְעָלָה מִן הָאָרֶץ:

mentioned. The Midrash (*Bereishis Rabbah* 94:9) explains that the missing number might be Yaakov, Yocheved, Hashem, **Serach bas Asher** (who is considered so significant that she is counted as two people, *Etz Yosef*), or **Chushim ben Dan** (who is counted as two since he had a brother not mentioned by name, *Maharzu*).

There are eight ways *Bnei Yisrael* stayed separate from the Egyptians. What are they?

They did not change 1) their names, 2) their language, 3) their clothing, or 4) their food. Additionally, 5) they did not intermarry, 6) they did not speak *lashon hara*, 7) they kept *bris milah*, and 8) they had *emunah* in Hashem (*Vayikra Rabbah* 32:5; *Midrash Lekach Tov* 6:6; *Midrash Lekach Tov Devarim* 26:5; *and Pirkei d'Rebbi Eliezer* 48). [Although we find sources indicating that the Jews did not keep *bris milah* (*Shemos Rabbah* 1:8), the *Beis HaLevi* in *Parashas Shemos* explains that, in truth, they did keep it, but they tried covering their *bris milah* to look as if they did not have one, mistakenly thinking that such a step would reduce the animosity the Egyptians felt toward them].

AND numerous—as it says: "I made you as numerous as the plants of the field; you increased and grew and you came to have great charm, beautiful of figure and your hair sprouting, but you were naked and bare." "I passed by you and saw you wallowing in your blood, and I said to you, 'By your blood you shall live!' I said to you, 'By your blood you shall live!' " (Yechezkel 16:7,6).

THE Egyptians did evil to us and afflicted us, and forced hard labor upon us (Devarim 26:6).

THE Egyptians did evil to us—as it says: "Come, let us deal wisely with them, lest they multiply and when there is a war they will join our enemies and fight us, and leave the land" (Shemos 1:10).

What did we do to deserve נִסִּים גְּלוּיִם—revealed miracles?

If a person does mitzvos with *mesirus nefesh* (self-sacrifice) and goes against his own nature to perform them, Hashem will in turn change the nature of the world for him. Therefore, Hashem gave the Jews two mitzvos with which to merit the *geulah: Korban Pesach* and *bris milah*. Sacrificing the *Korban Pesach* was done with great self-sacrifice—since sheep were worshipped by the Egyptians—and performing *bris milah* on oneself also demands a lot of courage, as it is not easy to wound oneself in such a manner. Those two mitzvos performed with *mesirus nefesh* would be the catalysts to allow *Bnei Yisrael* to leave Mitzrayim as free people (Rav Shlomo Zalman Auerbach in *Haggadas Arzei Levanon*).

How did the Egyptians succeed in making the Jews into bad people?

וַיָּרֵעוּ אֹתָנוּ can be understood to mean that the Egyptians made us evil people. This was accomplished by making the Jews poor, as the Gemara says (Eiruvin 41b), "Extreme poverty can make a person go against the words of Hashem" (Ya'avetz).

וַיְעַנּוּנוּ, כְּמָה שֶׁנֶּאֱמַר, וַיָּשִׂימוּ עָלָיו שָׂרֵי מִסִּים לְמַעַן עַנֹּתוֹ בְּסִבְלֹתָם, וַיִּבֶן עָרֵי מִסְכְּנוֹת לְפַרְעֹה אֶת פִּתֹם וְאֶת רַעַמְסֵס:

וַיִּתְּנוּ עָלֵינוּ עֲבֹדָה קָשָׁה, כְּמָה שֶׁנֶּאֱמַר, וַיַּעֲבִדוּ מִצְרַיִם אֶת בְּנֵי יִשְׂרָאֵל בְּפָרֶךְ:

וַנִּצְעַק אֶל יהוה אֱלֹהֵי אֲבֹתֵינוּ וַיִּשְׁמַע יהוה אֶת קֹלֵנוּ וַיַּרְא אֶת עָנְיֵנוּ וְאֶת עֲמָלֵנוּ וְאֶת לַחֲצֵנוּ:

What is the connection between property taxes and our enslavement?

Pharaoh collected taxes from property the Jews held in Eretz Canaan. He was therefore scared that the Jews would rebel against him and leave his country (*Shemos* 1:10). This was why he started to enslave them, to ensure that they would not rebel against him (*Ba'alei Tosefos*).

Who had to work their way to a debt-free life?

The שָׂרֵי מִסִּים—the Egyptian taskmasters—would impose heavy taxes on the Jews, so much so that the Jews fell into deep debt, which they were unable to repay. The Egyptians decided to enslave them to make them pay up their debts (Maharil Diskin).

How did the Egyptians succeed in creating machlokes amongst the Jewish people?

Some say that the שָׂרֵי מִסִּים were Jews appointed to the positions of taskmasters. This was done in order to foster ill will, jealousy, and *machlokes* among the Jews. The objective was to create strife within the Jewish nation, as the worst of tragedies happen when there is שִׂנְאַת חִנָם (baseless hatred) between fellow Jews (*Haggadas Rav Yonasan Eibeschutz*).

AND *afflicted us*—as it says: "And they placed taskmasters over them in order to afflict them with their burdens; and they built storage cities for Pharaoh—Pithom and Raamses" (Shemos 1:11).

AND *forced hard labor upon us*—as it is says: "And the Egyptians forced the Children of Israel to do crushing labor" (Shemos 1:13).

AND *we cried out to Hashem, the God of our fathers, and Hashem heard our voice and saw our affliction, our travail and our oppression* (Devarim 26:7).

One city mentioned in the Haggadah is made up of five letters with four נְקוּדוֹת (vowels). By changing which נְקוּדָה do you get an entirely different place?

The city Ramses is mentioned in *Bereishis* (47:11) and in *Shemos* (1:11). In *Bereishis*, this is the place where Yaakov and his family stayed when they first moved to Mitzrayim; in *Shemos* this is described as the city that the Jewish people were forced to build as slave laborers. The Ibn Ezra (in both places) explains that these are two completely different cities. The first one mentioned in *Bereishis* is spelled with a *sheva* under the letter *ayin*— רַעְמְסֵס —while the one in *Shemos* is spelled with a *patach* under the letter *ayin*— רַעַמְסֵס.

How does עֲבוֹדַת פֶּרֶךְ, slave labor, relate to one of the items in the Mishkan?

עֲבוֹדַת פֶּרֶךְ is related to the word פָּרוֹכֶת, which was the curtain in the Mishkan that separated the *Heichal* from the *Kodesh HaKodashim*. Likewise, the Egyptians separated husband and wife to prevent them from having more children in their efforts to harm the Jewish people's future (*Peirush HaMeyuchas l'Rashi*).

וַנִּצְעַק אֶל יְהוָה אֱלֹהֵי אֲבֹתֵינוּ, כְּמָה שֶׁנֶּאֱמַר, וַיְהִי בַיָּמִים הָרַבִּים הָהֵם וַיָּמָת מֶלֶךְ מִצְרַיִם וַיֵּאָנְחוּ בְנֵי יִשְׂרָאֵל מִן הָעֲבֹדָה וַיִּזְעָקוּ, וַתַּעַל שַׁוְעָתָם אֶל הָאֱלֹהִים מִן הָעֲבֹדָה:

וַיִּשְׁמַע יְהוָה אֶת קֹלֵנוּ, כְּמָה שֶׁנֶּאֱמַר, וַיִּשְׁמַע אֱלֹהִים אֶת נַאֲקָתָם, וַיִּזְכֹּר אֱלֹהִים אֶת בְּרִיתוֹ אֶת אַבְרָהָם אֶת יִצְחָק וְאֶת יַעֲקֹב:

וַיַּרְא אֶת עָנְיֵנוּ, זוֹ פְּרִישׁוּת דֶּרֶךְ אֶרֶץ, כְּמָה שֶׁנֶּאֱמַר, וַיַּרְא אֱלֹהִים אֶת בְּנֵי יִשְׂרָאֵל וַיֵּדַע אֱלֹהִים:

וְאֶת עֲמָלֵנוּ, אֵלּוּ הַבָּנִים, כְּמָה שֶׁנֶּאֱמַר, כָּל הַבֵּן הַיִּלּוֹד הַיְאֹרָה תַּשְׁלִיכֻהוּ וְכָל הַבַּת תְּחַיּוּן:

וְאֶת לַחֲצֵנוּ, זֶה הַדְּחַק, כְּמָה שֶׁנֶּאֱמַר, וְגַם רָאִיתִי אֶת הַלַּחַץ אֲשֶׁר מִצְרַיִם לֹחֲצִים אֹתָם:

Why did Pharaoh think that Levi was a great patriot?

Levi did not carry Yaakov's coffin when he was carried out of Mitzrayim to be buried in Eretz Canaan. This was based on Yaakov's final instructions before he passed away. However, Pharaoh mistakenly assumed that Levi was motivated by nationalistic intentions, and that Levi refused to carry Yaakov's body since he objected to burial outside of Mitzrayim. As a reward for Levi's loyalty to his country, Pharaoh exempted Levi's entire *shevet* from being slaves (*Ohr HaTorah*).

It looks like he is crying over X, but really he is crying over Y...

"When the king of Mitzrayim died, the Jewish people cried out due to their slave labor" (Shemos 2:23). The question is, why did they not cry out

AND *we cried out to Hashem, the God of our fathers* — *as it says: "It happened during those long days that the king of Egypt died, and the Children of Israel groaned because of the labor, and they cried out. And their plea from their labor ascended to God" (Shemos 2:23).*

AND *Hashem heard our voice* — *as it says: "And God heard their groaning, and God remembered His covenant with Avraham, with Yitzchak, and with Yaakov" (ibid. 2:24).*

AND *saw our affliction* — *This refers to the disruption of family life, as it says: "God saw the Children of Israel, and God knew" (ibid. 2:25).*

AND *our travail* — *This refers to the children, as it says: "Every boy that is born you shall throw into the river, but spare all the daughters" (ibid. 1:22).*

AND *our oppression* — *This refers to the pressure, as it is said: "And I have also seen the pressure with which the Egyptians oppress them" (ibid. 3:9).*

until the king died? One answer given is that they feared that screaming to Heaven about their situation could get them into further trouble from their taskmasters, and they therefore restrained themselves. However, when the king died and there were the customary eulogies with mourning and crying, the Jewish people also cried. To the untrained eye, it looked as though the Jewish people were crying over the loss of the king, while in truth they were crying over something completely different, namely, their slavery (*Shelah HaKadosh*).

From where do we learn that the Haggadah should be recited loud and clear?

The redemption from Mitzrayim came about through וַיִּשְׁמַע ה' אֶת קֹלֵנוּ,

וַיּוֹצִאֵנוּ יהוה מִמִּצְרַיִם בְּיָד חֲזָקָה וּבִזְרֹעַ נְטוּיָה וּבְמֹרָא גָּדֹל וּבְאֹתוֹת וּבְמֹפְתִים:

וַיּוֹצִאֵנוּ יהוה מִמִּצְרַיִם, לֹא עַל יְדֵי מַלְאָךְ וְלֹא עַל יְדֵי שָׂרָף וְלֹא עַל יְדֵי שָׁלִיחַ, אֶלָּא הַקָּדוֹשׁ בָּרוּךְ הוּא בִּכְבוֹדוֹ וּבְעַצְמוֹ, שֶׁנֶּאֱמַר, וְעָבַרְתִּי בְאֶרֶץ מִצְרַיִם בַּלַּיְלָה הַזֶּה, וְהִכֵּיתִי כָל בְּכוֹר בְּאֶרֶץ מִצְרַיִם מֵאָדָם וְעַד בְּהֵמָה וּבְכָל אֱלֹהֵי מִצְרַיִם אֶעֱשֶׂה שְׁפָטִים אֲנִי יהוה:

וְעָבַרְתִּי בְאֶרֶץ מִצְרַיִם בַּלַּיְלָה הַזֶּה, אֲנִי וְלֹא מַלְאָךְ: וְהִכֵּיתִי כָל בְּכוֹר בְּאֶרֶץ מִצְרַיִם, אֲנִי וְלֹא שָׂרָף: וּבְכָל אֱלֹהֵי מִצְרַיִם אֶעֱשֶׂה שְׁפָטִים, אֲנִי וְלֹא הַשָּׁלִיחַ: אֲנִי יהוה, אֲנִי הוּא וְלֹא אַחֵר:

בְּיָד חֲזָקָה, זוֹ הַדֶּבֶר, כְּמָה שֶׁנֶּאֱמַר, הִנֵּה יַד יהוה הוֹיָה בְּמִקְנְךָ אֲשֶׁר בַּשָּׂדֶה בַּסּוּסִים בַּחֲמֹרִים בַּגְּמַלִּים בַּבָּקָר וּבַצֹּאן, דֶּבֶר כָּבֵד מְאֹד:

Hashem heard our voice, when we cried out to Hashem. To express our gratitude to Hashem for saving us, we likewise need to do it בְּקוֹל רָם, in a loud and clear voice (*Seder Ha'Aruch*, p. 201).

How large and spacious was the land of Goshen?

It was not very large. The land of Goshen was given to Yaakov and his family when they came down to Mitzrayim as a group of seventy people. Later on in time, the Jewish people would multiply many times over due to a large birthrate. The Egyptians still did not let the

AND *Hashem took us out of Egypt with a strong hand and an outstretched arm, and with great awe, and with signs, and with wonders (Devarim 26:8).*

AND *Hashem took us out of Egypt*—*not through an angel, not through a seraph and not through an agent, but The Holy One, Blessed is He, in His glory, by Himself. Thus it says: "I will pass through the land of Egypt on that night, and I will strike every firstborn in the land of Egypt from man to beast, and against all the gods of Egypt I will mete out judgments, I am Hashem" (Shemos 12:12). I will pass through the land of Egypt on that night—I and not an angel; and I will strike every firstborn in the land of Egypt—I and not a seraph; and against all the gods of Egypt I will mete out judgments—I and not an agent; I am Hashem—it is I, and no one else.*

WITH *a strong hand*—*This refers to the pestilence, as it says: "Behold, the hand of Hashem will be upon your livestock in the field, upon the horses, the donkeys, the camels, the cattle, and the sheep, [with] a very severe pestilence" (ibid. 9:3).*

Jews settle outside of Goshen. This is what is meant by זֶה הַדְּחַק—the cramped feelings of being in a small, overcrowded area (*Rabbeinu Bachya, Shemos* 3:9).

Which conversation between Hashem and the angels was said at this point in some versions of the Haggadah?

The *Machzor Vitry* (*Hilchos Pesach* 95) quotes a conversation between Hashem and the angels, mentioned in the Haggadah in France:

> The angels said to Hashem, "It will not be befitting to go down by Yourself to Mitzrayim to do makkas Bechoros. Rather, we will do it for You. Just like a human king of flesh and blood

וּבִזְרֹעַ נְטוּיָה, זוֹ הַחֶרֶב, כְּמָה שֶׁנֶּאֱמַר, וְחַרְבּוֹ שְׁלוּפָה בְּיָדוֹ נְטוּיָה עַל יְרוּשָׁלָיִם:

וּבְמֹרָא גָּדֹל, זוֹ גִילּוּי שְׁכִינָה, כְּמָה שֶׁנֶּאֱמַר, אוֹ הֲנִסָּה אֱלֹהִים לָבוֹא לָקַחַת לוֹ גוֹי מִקֶּרֶב גּוֹי בְּמַסֹּת בְּאֹתֹת וּבְמוֹפְתִים וּבְמִלְחָמָה וּבְיָד חֲזָקָה וּבִזְרוֹעַ נְטוּיָה וּבְמוֹרָאִים גְּדֹלִים כְּכֹל אֲשֶׁר עָשָׂה לָכֶם יהוה אֱלֹהֵיכֶם בְּמִצְרַיִם לְעֵינֶיךָ:

וּבְאֹתֹות, זֶה הַמַּטֶּה, כְּמָה שֶׁנֶּאֱמַר, וְאֶת הַמַּטֶּה הַזֶּה תִּקַּח בְּיָדֶךָ אֲשֶׁר תַּעֲשֶׂה בּוֹ אֶת הָאֹתֹת:

It is customary to spill out some wine from the cup while saying the three terms: blood, fire and pillars of smoke

וּבְמוֹפְתִים, זֶה הַדָּם, כְּמָה שֶׁנֶּאֱמַר, וְנָתַתִּי מוֹפְתִים בַּשָּׁמַיִם וּבָאָרֶץ

דָּם וָאֵשׁ וְתִימְרוֹת עָשָׁן:

is surrounded by his officers when he goes to war so that no pain afflicts him, in the same way we want to carry out the job instead of You."

Hashem, however, did not accept the malachim's offer, and He Himself went down to Mitzrayim.

The *Machzor Vitry* says that one should not say this as part of the Haggadah, as it implies that Hashem could be subject to physical pain (if He would be "injured" in Mitzrayim), which is not correct, as

AND *with an outstretched arm* — This refers to the sword, as it says: "His sword was drawn in his hand, stretched out over Jerusalem" (I Divrei Hayamim 21:16).

AND *with great awe* — This refers to the revelation of the Divine Presence, as it says: "Or has any god ever attempted to go and take for himself a nation from the midst of another nation, with trials, signs, and wonders, with wars and with a strong hand and an outstretched arm and with great terrors, like all that Hashem your God did for you in Egypt before your eyes?" (Devarim 4:34).

AND *with signs* — This refers to the staff, as it says: "Take this staff in your hand, with which you shall perform the signs" (Shemos 4:17).

It is customary to spill out some wine from the cup while saying the three terms: blood, fire, and pillars of smoke

AND *with wonders* — This refers to the blood, as it says: "And I shall place wonders in heaven and on earth — **blood and fire and pillars of smoke**" (Yoel 3:3).

Hashem is not subject to physical pain. It is therefore no longer said today in our version of the Haggadah.

What do we refer to when we say דָּם וָאֵשׁ וְתִמְרוֹת עָשָׁן, blood, fire, and a pillar of smoke?

When the Jewish people *shechted* the *Korban Pesach*, they placed the **blood** on their doorposts and lintels, and they roasted the meat of the *Korban Pesach* over **fire**, which caused a **pillar of smoke**. For the Egyptians to see their own idol treated in such a way was like another plague, as they were powerless to rescue their own god (*HaShir V'HaShevach*).

דָם

Which waters in Mitzrayim did not turn into blood?

Only drinking water turned into blood, not salty or bitter waters (Rav Saadya Gaon, quoted in *Malbim* 7:22). Underground waters and water that was collected in utensils, pits, and cisterns before the plague started also did not turn to blood according to Rav Yehudah (*Shemos Rabbah* 9:11; *Etz Yosef*, ibid.). Perhaps the first of the plagues came with a few moderations to serve as a mild warning to the Egyptians to free the Jews. However, the plagues eventually escalated due to Pharaoh's refusal to let the Jewish people go.

In what way was the plague of Blood worse than the מַבּוּל (the Flood)?

During the מַבּוּל, the fish did not die, whereas in the plague of Blood, the fish did die (*Midrash Lekach Tov* 7:18).

In what way was Pharaoh rewarded during the plague of Blood for raising Moshe in his house?

Pharaoh was not affected by the plague of Blood (*Mishnas Rav Eliezer* 19). Perhaps the reason is because Pharaoh raised Moshe in his house and thereby gave him life, and in turn Pharaoh was rewarded with water, the essential ingredient of life.

צְפַרְדֵעַ

An enormous frog emerged from the waters of the Nile. The Eyptians began to hit it, and as a result of each strike, the

frog expelled swarms of frogs (*Rashi* 8:2). What would have happened to Egypt if the huge frog would not have been hit?

Nothing. They brought this plague on themselves. We learn an important lesson from this: One should not publicly dispute and attack other groups ("hit the frog") that have false philosophies even if one has the best of intentions. Fighting and protesting leads to a lot more problems ("swarms of frogs"), whereas simply remaining quiet saves a person from a lot of trouble (Rav Itzeleh Volozhiner, son of Rav Chaim Volozhiner, *Sefer Techeles Mordechai*).

What were the Egyptians thinking as they watched thousands of frogs jump out of the river (according to the basic explanation of the text that all the frogs emerged at once from the river, as opposed to just one large frog)?

It appeared to the Egyptians that the dead Jewish baby boys they had thrown into the river were coming back in the form of screaming and damaging frogs to hurt the people who had drowned them (*Malbim* 7:25).

What effect did the saliva of the frogs have on the economic situation in Egypt?

The *Midrash Tanchuma* (*Bo*) explains that the frogs were a punishment for the Egyptians for forcing the Jewish people to carry their merchandise. As a result, the frogs came and spoiled their goods. The frogs accomplished this through secreting mucus, slime, and other such discharges from their mouths in a way that spoiled all the Egyptian stock (*Kol HaRamaz*, ibid.).

Why did Pharaoh immediately harden his heart after Hashem removed all the frogs (8:11)?

Moshe cried out to Hashem concerning the frogs that He had inflicted upon Pharaoh (8:8), implying that he only asked Hashem to remove the frogs from Pharaoh's household. However, in reality, that is not what happened, as all the frogs died *from the houses, from the courtyards, and from the fields* (8:9). Once Pharaoh saw that Moshe's *tefillah* was not

answered exactly as Moshe had requested, he used that as an excuse to harden his heart (*Netziv* 8:11).

כְּנִים

What weapon can we compare the plague of Lice to?

Hashem threw spears at the Egyptians, these are the lice [who were sting-ing them like spears] (Midrash Tanchuma, Bo).

Who tried administering lice-removal medicine?

It says that Pharaoh's sorcerers also tried to create lice (לְהוֹצִיא אֶת הַכִּנִּים), but they were not successful (8:14). However, the *Malbim* translates the words לְהוֹצִיא אֶת הַכִּנִּים as *removing the lice*. In other words, the sorcerers tried eliminating the lice from the people and the animals by applying conventional ointments, etc., designed to remove the lice, but they were not successful (*Malbim* ibid.).

Why did Pharaoh harden his heart immediately after the plague of Lice, when his sorcerers said, "It is the finger of G-d"?

The *Malbim* translates the words אֶצְבַּע אֱלֹהִים, *finger of god* (8:15) to refer to an idol and not to Hashem. Thus, the sorcerers were really say-ing that this plague, since it arrived without a warning, came from an idol and not from Hashem. As a result, Pharaoh hardened his heart.

עָרוֹב

Which animals in particular fit the description of עָרוֹב—wild animals?

The word עָרוֹב is related to the word עֶרֶב (evening). This tells us that the plague consisted of animals who are active at night (in *Yirmiyahu*

5:6 and *Tzefanyah* 3:3, wolves are called *evening wolves* because they hunt at night) (see Rashbam 8:17).

What changes in Pharaoh's morning schedule happened after the plague of Blood?

Before the plague of Blood, Hashem told Moshe to go to Pharaoh in the morning (7:15). After that encounter, Pharaoh changed his daily routine to waking up even earlier (at dawn) so he should not have to meet Moshe again at the river. This is why Hashem told Moshe to *arise early* in the morning (8:16) to warn Pharaoh about the plague of the Wild Animals, to make sure he would still meet Pharaoh there (*Netziv* 8:16).

What was the only option the Egyptians had to save themselves from the Wild Animals?

...and the houses of Egypt shall be filled with the wild animals, and even the ground upon which they are (8:17). This teaches us that the animals would occupy not just the houses of the Egyptians, but even their empty land as well. Therefore, the only way the Egyptians could save themselves would be to escape to the land of Goshen, where the animals would not be found (8:18) (*Netziv* 8:17).

How did the plague of Wild Animals create friendship between Jews and Egyptians?

The Egyptians sought refuge from the wild animals in the land of Goshen, and as such they became friendly with the Jewish people. When Hashem told Moshe, *"Speak in the ears of the people, and let each man request from his friend and each woman from her friend silver vessels and gold vessels"* (11:2), it was clear that they had friends. These friendships came about through the plague of Wild Animals (*Netziv* 8:19).

Why does the Torah stress (8:18) *"I shall set apart the land of Goshen [from being attacked by the Wild Animals]"* more so than by any of the other *makkos*?

Since the plague of Wild Animals entailed that the animals surrounding

Mitzrayim would enter the country and damage it, many animals had to walk through the land of Goshen to get to Mitzrayim—yet they did no harm there (*Maharil Diskin* 8:18).

Why is the plague of Wild Animals called עָרוֹב, which literally means mixture/mingling?

The other *makkos* are named after the actual plague itself. The plague of עָרוֹב, however, is not named after the animals, but after the *combination* of the animals—different animals of the world all came together to cause great upheaval. Some animals need a tropical climate in which to survive, whereas others need an arctic climate. Each animal brought with it its environment and weather and thus affected the Egyptians with a great plague of constant climate changes. To remember this point, the plague is called עָרוֹב, reminding us of the multitude of animals (*Borchi Nafshi*, p. 149).

דֶּבֶר

Why was the warning Moshe gave Pharaoh concerning the plague of Pestilence more elaborate than those of the other plagues?

Concerning the other *makkos* that Pharaoh was warned about (Blood, Frogs, Wild Animals, Hail, and Grasshoppers), Moshe was commanded וְאָמַרְתָּ אֵלָיו, *you should say to him*. In this plague of Pestilence, the language used is וְדִבַּרְתָּ אֵלָיו, *you should speak to him*, connoting a longer, more in-depth warning. Why? By the other plagues, Pharaoh could change his heart in the middle and ask for the *makkah* to be reverted. This was not possible during the plague of Pestilence, as once the animals were dead, there was no going back.

Therefore, Moshe warned Pharaoh extensively about the impending plague (*Malbim* 9:1).

From the plague of Pestilence and onward, every single *makkah* directly affected...

The animals of the Egyptians. The plague of Pestilence killed animals, Boils were on the animals, Hail hit the animals, Locusts ate all of the vegetation on the ground, which the animals depended on for food, Darkness prevented the animals from getting food, and the Killing of the Firstborn applied to animals as well. In addition, *Bnei Yisrael* were commanded to take a sheep, slaughter it for the *Korban Pesach*, and place the blood on their doorposts for the public to see (*Bechor Shor* 9:5). The above plagues affected the animals because the Egyptians worshipped animals as idols.

We find that the Egyptians would not eat sheep (*Bereishis* 43:32). *Rashi* (8:22) explains that they would worship the actual animals as idols, while *Tosefos Hadar Zekeinim* states that they would form their idols to look like sheep, and as a sign of respect for their idol, they would therefore not eat actual sheep.

From where did the Jews get all the animals that they took with them when they left Mitzrayim?

Before the plague of Pestilence, the *pasuk* writes (9:5), *Hashem has set an appointed time, saying, "Tomorrow Hashem shall carry out this word in the land."* This message was communicated to the Egyptians. In this way, they would agree to sell their livestock to the Jews at a cheap rate, as otherwise the animals would die in the plague. In this way, the Jewish people ended up with a large amount of animals when they left Mitzrayim (*Netziv* 9:5). The *Meshech Chochmah* (ibid.) agrees that the Egyptians sold their livestock to *Bnei Yisrael*. However, he adds, *Bnei Yisrael* decided to show compassion after the plague of Pestilence and return all those animals back to the Egyptians. The *Meshech Chochmah* further explains that this was the reason the Egyptians so graciously parted with their clothing

and precious utensils when asked to do so by the Jews (11:3). They simply could not look the Jews in the eyes and deny their request after the Jewish people had given back the animals that they had legally bought.

The Kesav Sofer (12:38) explains that Pharaoh intentionally left them with their large amount of livestock when they became slaves and did not take away their possessions. Thus, these animals were always owned by *Bnei Yisrael*. The reason Pharaoh did not take them away was a sinister one: he knew that the degradation of a wealthy person forced to do slave labor is worse than that of a poor person. He therefore let them keep their wealth so they would be "wealthy" slaves, thus humiliating them further.

Where on the body did Pharaoh's sorcerers get Boils?

The sorcerers could not **stand** *before Moshe because of the boils...* (9:11). This teaches us that they were affected on their knees and thighs, so they literally could not stand in front of Moshe (see *Devarim* 28:35 that a punishment of boils is described as being on the knees and thighs) (*Bechor Shor* ibid.).

Who was subject to a harsher measure of Boils?

One who had a contagious case of *Shechin* would be isolated from others to prevent it from spreading (like we find that people with *tzara'as* also had to be quarantined). Since the sorcerers of Pharaoh degraded Hashem, it is likely that they were punished with a greater measure of Boils so that people would stay away from them. Boils is the only plague where the Torah describes the suffering of Pharaohs' sorcerers (*Chochmas Shlomo, Ruach Chein* 12).

Who had a previous history of skin disease and yet did not get Boils?

Pharaoh's sorcerers tried to inflict Moshe with boils but were unsuccessful. At the burning bush, Moshe had received *tzara'as* (4:6), and he was therefore more susceptible to catching other skin ailments. The fact that the sorcerers were still unable to give Moshe the boils was a cause of great embarrassment to them (*Meshech Chochmah* 9:11).

בָּרָד

What was the weather like in Mitzrayim just before the plague of Hail started?

It was sunny! Normally, hail comes from heavy clouds, but in this case, to show that it was a miraculous event, the weather was beautiful and sunny. This explains Moshe's warning to Pharaoh when he scratched a line in the wall and said, *"When the sun comes to this line tomorrow, the plague will start"* (*Rashi* 9:18, *Be'er Yosef*).

In what way was the *makkah* of Hail worse than all the other *makkos*?

The Hail destroyed all ripe grains (9:31) and thus caused a separate plague of hunger, which is worse than anything else (*Moshav Zekeinim*, see *Rashi* 9:14).

Which part of the plague of Hail occurred in the land of Goshen as well?

The *pasuk* states that *"Hashem sent thunder and hail"* (9:23) and *"Only in the land of Goshen, where the Bnei Yisrael were, there was no hail"* (9:26). This implies that there *was* thunder in the land of Goshen even

if there was no hail. The reason the thunder was heard in Goshen as well is because, according to the Gemara in *Berachos* 59a, the purpose of thunder is to straighten out the crookedness of a man's heart. Since there were Jews who were following the idolatrous ways of the Egyptians, they needed a reminder (in the form of thunder) to leave their evil ways and return to Hashem (*Netziv* 9:26).

Where was Moshe's shul?

When Pharaoh asked Moshe to stop the plague of Hail, Moshe said (9:29), *"When I leave the city I shall spread out my hands to Hashem."* Rashi comments that he could not daven inside the city, as it was filled with idols. Regarding the plagues of Frogs and Wild Animals, we also find that Moshe davened, but the Torah does not mention *where* he davened. Why does the Torah mention it only now, during the plague of Hail? The *Netziv* answers that Moshe had his own shul inside Mitzrayim where he would go to daven to Hashem (see 5:22, *"Moshe returned to Hashem and said..."*—he returned to a place specially designated for *tefillah* to "meet" Hashem). Inside his בֵּית הַכְּנֶסֶת, Moshe Rabbeinu davened for the plagues of Frogs and Wild Animals to end. The fact that there were idols in the streets did not pose a problem, since Moshe was inside the shul. However, during the plague of Hail, Moshe had to lift up his hands toward the heavens to stop the plague, and he therefore could not be inside his בֵּית הַכְּנֶסֶת. However, outside he encountered the idols of the Egyptians, and as a result he had to leave the city in order to daven, as he could not daven in a place filled with idols (*Netziv* 9:29).

When did Pharaoh admit to killing innocent Egyptians?

Regarding the plague of Hail, it says (9:19) that Pharaoh was warned that any animal or person found in the field would be killed. Pharaoh admitted afterward that he had not taken the warning seriously, and as a result both people and animals died in the plague (9:25). That is what Pharaoh meant when he said *"This time I have sinned"* (9:27),

meaning, this time I have spilled the blood of innocent Egyptians while *"Hashem is the righteous one"* (ibid.) for warning me first (*Malbim 9:27*).

When in history did the קוֹלֹת וּבְרָקִים, *thunder and lightning* heard at the plague of Hail occur again?

At מַתַּן תּוֹרָה! When asked to pray for the plague of Hail to stop, Moshe Rabbeinu said to Pharaoh, *"When I leave the city I shall spread out my hands to Hashem, the thunder will cease and the hail will no longer be"* (9:29). It does not say that the **thunder** will *no longer be*, only that it will cease, whereas the *pasuk* says the **hail** will *no longer be*. This implies that the thunder would occur again in history, while the hail would never happen again. (The hail-stones described in *Yehoshua* 10:11 were not as miraculous as the plague of Hail [*Moshav Zekeinim*].) The thunder did indeed happen again—at מַתַּן תּוֹרָה, where we find that the Torah was given amidst thunderous sounds (9:16) (*Pa'anei'ach Raza*).

אַרְבֶּה

Which plague did Moshe get to choose?

Hashem told Moshe what each *makkah* would be before they happened—except for the plague of Grasshoppers. The first time Grasshoppers are mentioned is when Moshe tells Pharaoh about the impending plague. The Chasam Sofer explains that Hashem allowed Moshe to choose whichever plague he wanted for the eighth one, and Moshe selected the plague of Grasshoppers.

(However, others explain that Hashem did in fact communicate to Moshe which plague He was about to bring on Mitzrayim. Since Hashem had just told Moshe [10:2] that he should tell over

the story of the *makkos* to his son, Moshe understood that the next *makkah* was referring to the plague of Grasshoppers. Why? Since grasshoppers were a rather common occurrence throughout history, any time they would come it would serve as a reminder for *Bnei Yisrael* to talk about the great plague of Grasshoppers in Mitzrayim—"You think this is a lot of grasshoppers? This is nothing compared to the grasshoppers we saw in Mitzrayim!" [*Bechor Shor*]).

How does the name אַרְבֶּה (Grasshoppers)
show the מִדָה כְּנֶגֶד מִדָה of this plague?

The Egyptians wanted to terminate the *berachah* of וָאַרְבֶּה אֶת זַרְעוֹ, *and I will multiply his children* (*Yehoshua* 24:3) that was promised to Avraham Avinu. They did so by actively killing the Jewish children and preventing the births of many more. Therefore, Hashem brought the Grasshoppers, which are called אַרְבֶּה, to destroy all the Egyptians' crops (*Chida, Rosh David*).

How does the plague of Grasshoppers testify that
all the plagues were directly from Hashem?

Although it is clear from all the *makkos* that Hashem guides, directs, and controls all affairs of the world, the plague of Grasshoppers provides more conclusive evidence. After the plague of Grasshoppers, Egypt was finished. The country had suffered devastating blows with Hail and Grasshoppers, which completely wiped out every last bit of crop in the land. How could Pharaoh **not** let *Bnei Yisrael* go at this point? The only explanation is that Hashem hardened Pharaoh's heart (as a punishment for originally misusing his free will, see *Rambam, Hilchos Teshuvah* 6:3). Since only Hashem can intervene to remove man's free choice, this was clearly an act of Hashem, teaching us that all the *makkos* were truly Hashem's doing (*Kesav Sofer*).

חֹשֶׁךְ

On which date did the wicked Jews die?

We know that the *resha'im* among the Jews died during the plague of Darkness (see *Rashi* 13:18). The date was the thirteenth of Adar. Later in history, Haman drew lots to choose a day to murder the Jews, and when his lot fell on the thirteenth of Adar, he felt it was an auspicious day, since previously so many Jewish people had died in Mitzrayim on that date. וּלְכָל בְּנֵי יִשְׂרָאֵל הָיָה אוֹר בְּמוֹשְׁבֹתָם, *but for all Bnei Yisrael there was light in their dwellings* (10:23) — the gematria of the word אוֹר equals בַּאֲדָר, which indicates that the plague of Darkness happened in the month of Adar (see *Chida* in *Chomas Anach*).

What can the bat teach us about the plague of Darkness?

During the day, bats are blinded by the sun's rays, and they perceive everything around them as dark. The same thing happened during the plague of Darkness. It came about by Hashem sending forth a brilliant spiritual light that was brighter than anything we are familiar with. This heavenly glow blinded the eyes of the Egyptians and served as a light for the Jewish people, who were able to tolerate these radiant rays (*Shach al HaTorah, Sha'arei Aharon*, p. 268).

Why didn't Pharaoh ask Moshe to daven for the removal of Darkness?

Pharaoh thought that Darkness had enveloped all of Mitzrayim and that *Bnei Yisrael* were also subject to this plague, as he could not see anything indicating the contrary. Thus, he did not think it was a specific plague from Hashem, so he did not ask Moshe to daven for it to be removed (*Moshav Zekeinim* 11:24).

מַכַּת בְּכוֹרוֹת

Where do we find that pollution kills?

מַכַּת בְּכוֹרוֹת happened through polluted air that Hashem brought to Mitzrayim. This air entered into the mouth and nostrils of the firstborns and went directly to their heart, killing them. In Hashem's miraculous kindness, those firstborn Jews who had the blood of the *Korban Pesach* on their doors were not affected by this *makkah* (*Abarbanel* 12:3).

Which Egyptians were not punished with מַכַּת בְּכוֹרוֹת?

Pharaoh's soldiers were not included in the plague of the Firstborn, since members of the army do not have any superiority over others by virtue of their being firstborns (as opposed to family members living together). Therefore, the firstborns serving in the army did not really have firstborn status. The members of Pharaoh's army were all punished later, at the Yam Suf (*Netziv* 12:30).

How exactly did Pharaoh give the Jews permission to leave?

Pharaoh called to Moshe and Aharon during the night after the plague of the Firstborn and said, *"Rise up, go out from among my people"* (12:31). The *mesorah* teaches us that the word צְּאוּ, *go out* has a *dagesh* in the letter (although grammatically the letter צ does not usually get a *dagesh*). The word צְאוּ without a *dagesh* would mean that Pharaoh simply gave his permission for them to leave but did not force them to do so. The *dagesh* spelling tells us that Pharaoh gave strict orders to "get out of here quickly, I do not want you around any longer!" (*Netziv* 12:31).

What did the Jews pray for on the night of the Exodus?

They asked Hashem to spare them from מַכַּת בְּכוֹרוֹת. Although they had been promised that Hashem would pass over their houses, they

nevertheless feared that they might have done *aveiros* in the interim, which could lead Hashem to go back on His promise. Based on that *tefillah* that was said in Mitzrayim, we also say the *tefillah* of הַשְׁכִּיבֵנוּ every night, asking Hashem to protect us from dangers (Rabbeinu Yonah, *Berachos* 2b).

Whom did the Jews pray for at Har Sinai?

After the plague of the Firstborn, Pharaoh said to Moshe and Aharon, *"And bless me as well"* (12:32). The *Netziv* suggests that there is no reason to assume that Moshe would not fulfill Pharaoh's request—since we don't find any indication that Moshe objected, it can be understood that he agreed to honor it. The place most conducive for blessing Pharaoh would be at Har Sinai, because that is where *Bnei Yisrael* first served Hashem and brought *korbanos* [it is known from the Midrash that Pharaoh survived the ordeal at the Yam Suf and was therefore still alive at the time of *Matan Torah*]. However, it is possible that Moshe retracted his commitment, and that would have been due to Pharaoh's change of heart when he pursued *Bnei Yisrael* after they left Mitzrayim (*Netziv* 12:32).

Which of the makkos affected the Jews as well?

All of the plagues affected the Jewish people for a short span of time so they should know the strength of the *makkos* being inflicted upon the Egyptians. This is seen from the *pasuk* (10:23) *"...but for all Bnei Yisrael there was light in their dwellings."* This implies that the Jews experienced the joy of having light after being exposed to darkness for a short while. This phenomenon of first experiencing the plague occurred by the other *makkos* as well. (*Chida* in *Penei David*).

Which two makkos do we find specifically associated with the Yam Suf?

Hashem turned back a very powerful west wind and it carried the **locust swarm** *and hurled it toward the Yam Suf* (10:19). And before the splitting of the sea, the Torah writes that the Egyptians experienced *cloud and* **darkness** (14:20).

דָּבָר אַחֵר, בְּיָד חֲזָקָה שְׁתַּיִם, וּבִזְרֹעַ נְטוּיָה שְׁתַּיִם, וּבְמֹרָא גָדֹל שְׁתַּיִם, וּבְאֹתוֹת שְׁתַּיִם, וּבְמֹפְתִים שְׁתַּיִם: אֵלּוּ עֶשֶׂר מַכּוֹת שֶׁהֵבִיא הַקָּדוֹשׁ בָּרוּךְ הוּא עַל הַמִּצְרַיִם בְּמִצְרַיִם, וְאֵלּוּ הֵן —

Some wine is spilled out with the mention of each of the ten plagues, as well as the three words of Rabbi Yehudah's acronym.

דָּם, צְפַרְדֵּעַ, כִּנִּים, עָרוֹב, דֶּבֶר, שְׁחִין, בָּרָד, אַרְבֶּה, חֹשֶׁךְ, מַכַּת בְּכוֹרוֹת:

רַבִּי יְהוּדָה הָיָה נוֹתֵן בָּהֶם סִמָּנִים, דְּצַ"ךְ, עַדַ"שׁ, בְּאַחַ"ב:

What should a person do if he is unable to drink the wine after he dips his finger in it?

There are different *minhagim* regarding how one should spill out the wine from his cup when he recites the ten *makkos*; some hold it should be done with one's finger, and others say to pour it out of the cup. If a person is very sensitive (אִסְטָנִיס) and will not be able to drink the wine if he dips his finger into it, then he should pour the wine out of his cup (*Sha'ar HaTziyun* 573:81).

Rav Yehudah shortened the ten plagues to דְּצַ"ךְ עַדַ"שׁ בְּאַחַ"ב. The Haggadah of *Minhag Teiman* adds that Rav Levi used a different abbreviation: סְקַ"ח לַדַ"ן בְּכַחָ"ב. What does that stand for?

It is a mnemonic for the ten *makkos* as mentioned in the *Midrash Tanchuma* (*Bo*). The Midrash relates how the ten *makkos* parallel

ANOTHER *explanation of the verse is:* **With a strong hand** *indicates two plagues;* **with an outstretched arm** *indicates two plagues;* **with great terrors** *indicates two plagues;* **with signs** *indicates two plagues;* **and with wonders** *indicates two plagues. These are the ten plagues, which the Holy One, Blessed is He, brought upon the Egyptians:*

Some wine is spilled out with the mention of each of the ten plagues, as well as the three words of Rabbi Yehudah's acronym.

BLOOD, *Frogs, Lice, Wild Animals, Pestilence, Boils, Hail, Locusts, Darkness, the Plague of the Firstborn.*

RABBI *Yehudah used to combine their initials into an acronym:*

D'TzaCh, ADaSh, Be'AChaV.

the ten steps of warfare against an enemy that refuses to surrender. First Hashem closed the water flow (סָכַר אַמַת הַמַּיִם) by turning the water into blood; then He brought noisemakers (קְלָאנִים), in the form of frogs, to scare the enemy; then He threw spears at them (חִצִּים) with the attack of the lice; then He sent in an army division (לִגְיוֹנוֹת) of wild animals to strike them; then He brought an epidemic (דּוֹרְמַסְיוֹת) to kill their animals; then He confronted them with foul-smelling petroleum (נֵפְט), a result of putrid boils all over their bodies; then He hurled stones at them (בְּלִיסְטְרָאוֹת), in the form of hail; then He brought in His army of grasshoppers to dominate them (כּוֹבְשִׁים); then He imprisoned them in total darkness (חֲשֵׁיכָה); and, finally, He killed their prominent individuals by slaying the firstborns (בְּכוֹרוֹת).

The cups are refilled to replace the wine that was spilled out.

רַבִּי יוֹסֵי הַגְּלִילִי אוֹמֵר, מִנַּיִן אַתָּה אוֹמֵר שֶׁלָּקוּ הַמִּצְרִים בְּמִצְרַיִם עֶשֶׂר מַכּוֹת וְעַל הַיָּם לָקוּ חֲמִשִּׁים מַכּוֹת. בְּמִצְרַיִם מָה הוּא אוֹמֵר, וַיֹּאמְרוּ הַחַרְטֻמִּם אֶל פַּרְעֹה אֶצְבַּע אֱלֹהִים הִוא. וְעַל הַיָּם מָה הוּא אוֹמֵר, וַיַּרְא יִשְׂרָאֵל אֶת הַיָּד הַגְּדֹלָה אֲשֶׁר עָשָׂה יהוה בְּמִצְרַיִם וַיִּירְאוּ הָעָם אֶת יהוה וַיַּאֲמִינוּ בַּיהוה וּבְמֹשֶׁה עַבְדּוֹ: כַּמָּה לָקוּ בְּאֶצְבַּע עֶשֶׂר מַכּוֹת. אֱמֹר מֵעַתָּה, בְּמִצְרַיִם לָקוּ עֶשֶׂר מַכּוֹת וְעַל הַיָּם לָקוּ חֲמִשִּׁים מַכּוֹת:

רַבִּי אֱלִיעֶזֶר אוֹמֵר, מִנַּיִן שֶׁכָּל מַכָּה וּמַכָּה שֶׁהֵבִיא הַקָּדוֹשׁ בָּרוּךְ הוּא עַל הַמִּצְרִים בְּמִצְרַיִם הָיְתָה שֶׁל אַרְבַּע מַכּוֹת, שֶׁנֶּאֱמַר, יְשַׁלַּח בָּם חֲרוֹן אַפּוֹ עֶבְרָה וָזַעַם וְצָרָה מִשְׁלַחַת מַלְאֲכֵי רָעִים: עֶבְרָה, אַחַת. וָזַעַם, שְׁתַּיִם. וְצָרָה, שָׁלֹשׁ. מִשְׁלַחַת מַלְאֲכֵי רָעִים, אַרְבַּע. אֱמֹר מֵעַתָּה, בְּמִצְרַיִם לָקוּ אַרְבָּעִים מַכּוֹת וְעַל הַיָּם לָקוּ מָאתַיִם מַכּוֹת:

Who did the Jewish people fear the most when they stood at the Yam Suf?

Hashem had already told them, וְאִכָּבְדָה בְּפַרְעֹה וּבְכָל־חֵילוֹ, *And I will be glorified through Pharaoh and through his entire army* (14:4), so they knew they had nothing to fear from Pharaoh or his army. The fear came when the Jewish people saw וְהִנֵּה מִצְרַיִם נֹסֵעַ אַחֲרֵיהֶם, *Egypt was journeying after them* (14:10). A large number of the Egyptian populace

The cups are refilled to replace the wine that was spilled out.

RABBI *Yosi Haglili said: How can it be shown that the Egyptians suffered ten plagues in Egypt, and then suffered fifty plagues at the sea? What does it say about [the plagues of] Egypt? "The magicians said to Pharaoh: This is the finger of God" (Shemos 8:15). But when it comes to [the plagues of] the sea it says, "Israel saw the great hand that Hashem wielded against Egypt, and the people feared Hashem, and they believed in Hashem and in His servant Moshe" (ibid. 14:31). Now, how many plagues did they suffer by God's "finger"? Ten plagues! Hence, you may infer that in Egypt they suffered ten plagues, while at the sea they suffered fifty plagues!*

RABBI *Eliezer said: How can it be shown that each plague that the Holy One, Blessed is He, inflicted upon the Egyptians in Egypt actually consisted of four plagues? Because it says: "He sent against them the heat of His anger, wrath and fury and calamity, a delegation of agents of evil" (Tehillim 78:49): Wrath—one, fury—two, calamity—three, a delegation of agents of evil—four. Hence, you may infer that in Egypt they suffered forty plagues, while at the sea they suffered two hundred plagues.*

followed behind the army, and those commoners were not expected at all. The Jews were afraid of the multitude of the general populace, who had come to join the fight as well (*Netziv* ibid.)

What happened to the Egyptian masses that came to the Yam Suf?

They were divided into three groups. Many of them never even made it into the Yam Suf and just watched the whole spectacle from the

רַבִּי עֲקִיבָא אוֹמֵר, מִנַּיִן שֶׁכָּל מַכָּה וּמַכָּה שֶׁהֵבִיא
הַקָּדוֹשׁ בָּרוּךְ הוּא עַל הַמִּצְרִים בְּמִצְרַיִם הָיְתָה שֶׁל
חָמֵשׁ מַכּוֹת, שֶׁנֶּאֱמַר, יְשַׁלַּח בָּם חֲרוֹן אַפּוֹ עֶבְרָה וָזַעַם
וְצָרָה מִשְׁלַחַת מַלְאֲכֵי רָעִים: חֲרוֹן אַפּוֹ, אַחַת. עֶבְרָה,
שְׁתַּיִם. וָזַעַם, שָׁלֹשׁ. וְצָרָה, אַרְבַּע. מִשְׁלַחַת מַלְאֲכֵי
רָעִים, חָמֵשׁ. אֱמֹר מֵעַתָּה, בְּמִצְרַיִם לָקוּ חֲמִשִּׁים מַכּוֹת
וְעַל הַיָּם לָקוּ חֲמִשִּׁים וּמָאתַיִם מַכּוֹת:

sea shore, as only Pharaoh's army entered in full (14:23). A second
group was in the Yam Suf, but when the waters started returning to
normal, they escaped by swimming back to the shore (וַיֹּאמֶר מִצְרַיִם
אָנוּסָה מִפְּנֵי יִשְׂרָאֵל, *and Egypt said 'Let me escape before Israel'*—14:25).
The third group drowned in the Yam Suf (וְיָשֻׁבוּ הַמַּיִם עַל מִצְרַיִם, *the waters will return on Egypt*—14:26). Exactly who died and who survived
was an extraordinary act of Hashem's providence (הַשְׁגָּחָה פְּרָטִית), as
the Egyptians were punished according to their level of wickedness.
Likewise, the Egyptians who died did not all suffer the same fate, as
some were punished in harsher ways than others, all according to how
cruel they had been to the Jewish people. All this led the Jewish people to a heightened level of *emunah*, as it says, וַיַּאֲמִינוּ בַּה׳ וּבְמֹשֶׁה עַבְדּוֹ
(14:31) (*Netziv* ibid.).

Why did Hashem orchestrate that a large number of Egyptians would be present at the splitting of the Yam Suf?

To be made aware of Hashem's greatness. Until now, only Pharaoh and
his close advisors saw Moshe or Aharon perform the *makkos*. They also
witnessed Moshe's *tefillos* bring them to an end. The general populace
experienced the plagues, but did not watch them come about. Thus,
they did not fully internalize that these plagues were Divine messages.

RABBI *Akiva said: How can it be shown that each plague that the Holy One, Blessed is He, inflicted upon the Egyptians in Egypt actually consisted of five plagues? Because it says: "He sent against them the heat of His anger, wrath and fury and calamity, a delegation of agents of evil": The heat of His anger—one, wrath—two, fury—three, calamity—four, a delegation of agents of evil—five. Hence, you may infer that in Egypt they suffered fifty plagues, while at the sea they suffered two hundred and fifty plagues.*

Additionally, the plagues they experienced were also less severe than the plagues that affected Pharaoh and his advisors. They did not yet perceive the full sense of Hashem's retribution for the enslavement of the Jewish people until they came to witness the splitting of the Yam Suf.

Furthermore, after watching the splitting of the Yam Suf, they would understand that the Jewish people had no intention of ever returning to Egypt. Had they not watched the splitting of the Yam Suf, the Egyptians would have demanded that their possessions be returned. After seeing the Jewish people walk through the split sea, they understood that their belongings would not be returned to them (but would remain with the Jews as payment for their two hundred and ten years of slavery—Sanhedrin 91a) (*Netziv* 14:4 and 14:13).

Why couldn't the horses of the Egyptians just swim out of the waters to safety?

There were many foot soldiers in the way. The crowded conditions made escaping impossible (*Netziv* 14:28).

Yam Suf means the Sea of Reeds. The horses got entangled in the reeds and became stuck, unable to get themselves out of the waters (*Netziv* 15:4).

כַּמָּה מַעֲלוֹת טוֹבוֹת לַמָּקוֹם עָלֵינוּ:

אִלּוּ הוֹצִיאָנוּ מִמִּצְרַיִם וְלֹא עָשָׂה בָהֶם שְׁפָטִים, דַּיֵּנוּ.

אִלּוּ עָשָׂה בָהֶם שְׁפָטִים וְלֹא עָשָׂה בֵאלֹהֵיהֶם, דַּיֵּנוּ.

אִלּוּ עָשָׂה בֵאלֹהֵיהֶם וְלֹא הָרַג אֶת בְּכוֹרֵיהֶם, דַּיֵּנוּ.

אִלּוּ הָרַג אֶת בְּכוֹרֵיהֶם וְלֹא נָתַן לָנוּ אֶת מָמוֹנָם, דַּיֵּנוּ.

אִלּוּ נָתַן לָנוּ אֶת מָמוֹנָם וְלֹא קָרַע לָנוּ אֶת הַיָּם, דַּיֵּנוּ.

אִלּוּ קָרַע לָנוּ אֶת הַיָּם וְלֹא הֶעֱבִירָנוּ בְתוֹכוֹ בֶּחָרָבָה,
דַּיֵּנוּ.

אִלּוּ הֶעֱבִירָנוּ בְתוֹכוֹ בֶּחָרָבָה וְלֹא שִׁקַּע צָרֵינוּ בְּתוֹכוֹ,
דַּיֵּנוּ.

In some cases there was no apparent reason for this phenomenon, and even a light horse and rider would sink to the bottom of the sea like a heavy stone—יָרְדוּ בִמְצוֹלֹת כְּמוֹ-אָבֶן, *they went down to the bottom like a stone* (*Netziv* 15:5).

To enable the Jewish people to cross the Yam Suf, Hashem lifted up the bottom of the sea to make it level with the ground. When the time came for things to revert back to their original state, Hashem caused this "ground" to crash down to the seabed. The vast number of small stones that resulted from this blast floated in the waters and made escaping impossible (*Malbim* 15:5).

What miracle was equal to the splitting of the Yam Suf?

When Hashem split the sea for the Jewish people, He effected an actual change to the physical laws of water. This is what *Chazal* mean when they say that all waters in the world split at the time of

How grateful we must be to the Omnipresent for all the levels of kindness He has done for us!

If He had brought us out of Egypt, but not meted out judgments against them—it would have been sufficient for us!

If He had meted out judgments against them, but not against their gods—it would have been sufficient for us!

If He had done so against their gods, but not slain their first-born—it would have been sufficient for us!

If He had slain their firstborn, but not given us their money—it would have been sufficient for us!

If He had given us their money, but not split the sea for us—it would have been sufficient for us!

If He had split the sea for us, but had not led us through it on dry land—it would have been sufficient for us!

If He had led us through on dry land, but not submerged our enemies in it—it would have been sufficient for us!

Kri'as Yam Suf. When Hashem wanted the Egyptians to suffer their ultimate defeat in the waters of the Yam Suf, the original properties of water were needed. To effect that change, a miracle was necessary for water to revert to its original physical state. This is why Moshe Rabbeinu needed to *stretch out his hand* (14:26) to generate this miracle (*Malbim* 14:27).

Who gets pleasure from doing favors for others?

Hashem! The Haggadah should have said כַּמָה מַעֲלוֹת טוֹבוֹת מִמָּקוֹם עָלֵינוּ, *how many favors from Hashem to us*, and not כַּמָה מַעֲלוֹת טוֹבוֹת לַמָּקוֹם עָלֵינוּ, *how many favors to Hashem for us*. This teaches us that Hashem gets *nachas ruach* (pleasure) by bestowing His kindnesses on us (*Kedushas Levi*).

אִלּוּ שִׁקַּע צָרֵינוּ בְּתוֹכוֹ וְלֹא סִפֵּק צָרְכֵּנוּ בַּמִּדְבָּר אַרְבָּעִים שָׁנָה, דַּיֵּנוּ.

אִלּוּ סִפֵּק צָרְכֵּנוּ בַּמִּדְבָּר אַרְבָּעִים שָׁנָה וְלֹא הֶאֱכִילָנוּ אֶת הַמָּן, דַּיֵּנוּ.

אִלּוּ הֶאֱכִילָנוּ אֶת הַמָּן וְלֹא נָתַן לָנוּ אֶת הַשַּׁבָּת, דַּיֵּנוּ.

אִלּוּ נָתַן לָנוּ אֶת הַשַּׁבָּת וְלֹא קֵרְבָנוּ לִפְנֵי הַר סִינַי, דַּיֵּנוּ.

אִלּוּ קֵרְבָנוּ לִפְנֵי הַר סִינַי וְלֹא נָתַן לָנוּ אֶת הַתּוֹרָה, דַּיֵּנוּ.

אִלּוּ נָתַן לָנוּ אֶת הַתּוֹרָה וְלֹא הִכְנִיסָנוּ לְאֶרֶץ יִשְׂרָאֵל, דַּיֵּנוּ.

אִלּוּ הִכְנִיסָנוּ לְאֶרֶץ יִשְׂרָאֵל וְלֹא בָנָה לָנוּ אֶת בֵּית הַבְּחִירָה, דַּיֵּנוּ.

עַל אַחַת כַּמָּה וְכַמָּה טוֹבָה כְפוּלָה וּמְכֻפֶּלֶת לַמָּקוֹם עָלֵינוּ, שֶׁהוֹצִיאָנוּ מִמִּצְרַיִם, וְעָשָׂה בָהֶם שְׁפָטִים, וְעָשָׂה בֵאלֹהֵיהֶם, וְהָרַג אֶת בְּכוֹרֵיהֶם, וְנָתַן לָנוּ אֶת מָמוֹנָם, וְקָרַע לָנוּ אֶת הַיָּם, וְהֶעֱבִירָנוּ בְתוֹכוֹ בֶּחָרָבָה, וְשִׁקַּע צָרֵינוּ בְּתוֹכוֹ, וְסִפֵּק צָרְכֵּנוּ בַּמִּדְבָּר אַרְבָּעִים שָׁנָה, וְהֶאֱכִילָנוּ אֶת הַמָּן, וְנָתַן לָנוּ אֶת הַשַּׁבָּת, וְקֵרְבָנוּ לִפְנֵי הַר סִינַי, וְנָתַן לָנוּ אֶת הַתּוֹרָה, וְהִכְנִיסָנוּ לְאֶרֶץ יִשְׂרָאֵל, וּבָנָה לָנוּ אֶת בֵּית הַבְּחִירָה לְכַפֵּר עַל כָּל עֲוֹנוֹתֵינוּ:

Who wrote דַּיֵּנוּ, and when was it written?

Some say that דַּיֵּנוּ is a continuation of the words of Rabbi Akiva

If He had submerged our enemies in it, but not supplied our needs in the desert for forty years—it would have been sufficient for us!

If He had supplied our needs in the desert for forty years, but not fed us manna—it would have been sufficient for us!

If He had fed us manna, but not given us the Sabbath—it would have been sufficient for us!

If He had given us the Sabbath, but not brought us before Mount Sinai—it would have been sufficient for us!

If He had brought us before Mount Sinai, but not given us the Torah—it would have been sufficient for us!

If He had given us the Torah, but not taken us into the Land of Israel—it would have been sufficient for us!

If He had taken us into the land of Israel, but not built the Temple for us—it would have been sufficient for us!

HOW *much more so, then, must we be grateful to the Omnipresent for the manifold, repeated beneficence that He has bestowed upon us. For He brought us out of Egypt, meted out judgments against them, did so also against their gods, slew their firstborn, gave us their money, split the sea for us, led us through it on dry land, submerged our enemies in it, supplied our needs in the desert for forty years, fed us manna, gave us the Sabbath, brought us before Mount Sinai, gave us the Torah, took us into the Land of Israel, and built the Temple for us, to atone for all our sins.*

(who expounded upon the *makkos* the Egyptians received at the Yam Suf), and he, therefore, is the author of this *piyut* (*Zevach Pesach*). According to the *Rashbatz*, it was composed during the times of

רַבָּן גַּמְלִיאֵל הָיָה אוֹמֵר, כָּל שֶׁלֹּא אָמַר שְׁלֹשָׁה דְבָרִים אֵלּוּ בַּפֶּסַח לֹא יָצָא יְדֵי חוֹבָתוֹ, וְאֵלּוּ הֵן: פֶּסַח, מַצָּה, וּמָרוֹר:

When saying the words "The Pesach offering, which our ancestors ate," one should glance at the shank bone on the Seder plate. However, the shank bone should not be raised.

פֶּסַח שֶׁהָיוּ אֲבוֹתֵינוּ אוֹכְלִים בִּזְמַן שֶׁבֵּית הַמִּקְדָּשׁ הָיָה קַיָּם, עַל שׁוּם מָה. עַל שׁוּם שֶׁפָּסַח הַקָּדוֹשׁ בָּרוּךְ הוּא עַל בָּתֵּי אֲבוֹתֵינוּ בְּמִצְרָיִם. שֶׁנֶּאֱמַר, וַאֲמַרְתֶּם זֶבַח פֶּסַח הוּא לַיהוָה אֲשֶׁר פָּסַח עַל בָּתֵּי בְנֵי יִשְׂרָאֵל בְּמִצְרַיִם בְּנָגְפּוֹ אֶת מִצְרַיִם וְאֶת בָּתֵּינוּ הִצִּיל וַיִּקֹּד הָעָם וַיִּשְׁתַּחֲוּוּ:

the Beis HaMikdash, and it was used as a song of praise for one who brought *bikkurim*. The *Shibolei HaLeket*, however, says that it was composed after the destruction of the Beis HaMikdash, and it serves as the introduction to *Rabban Gamliel*, which talks about the Pesach offering that used to be eaten when the Beis HaMikdash was standing.

Which fifteen years in history were crucial in enabling us to leave Egypt?

For fifteen years, the three *Avos*—Avraham, Yitzchak, and Yaakov—concurrently spent time learning Torah together. It was in that זְכוּת that the Jewish people merited *Yetzias Mitzrayim*, and that is why there are fifteen steps in דַיֵּנוּ (*Chida* in *Midbar Kedeimos Alef*, quoting *talmidim* of Rav Yehudah HaChasid).

Why would someone conceivably skip saying רַבָּן גַּמְלִיאֵל הָיָה אוֹמֵר?

Rabban Gamliel used to say, Whoever does not say these three things on Pesach has not fulfilled his obligation: Pesach, matzah, and maror.

RABBAN *Gamliel used to say: Whoever does not talk about [the symbolism of] the following three things on Pesach has not fulfilled his obligation—the Pesach offering, matzah, and maror.*

When saying the words "The Pesach offering, which our ancestors ate," one should glance at the shank bone on the Seder plate. However, the shank bone should not be raised.

THE *Pesach offering, which our ancestors ate when the Temple was still standing—what does it represent? It represents the fact that the Holy One, Blessed is He, passed over our ancestors' houses in Egypt, as it says: "You shall say, It is a Pesach offering to Hashem, offered because He passed over the houses of the Children of Israel in Egypt when He smote the Egyptians, and He saved our houses. And the people bowed and prostrated themselves" (Shemos 12:27).*

There is a *machlokes* as to which mitzvah one has not fulfilled if he does not say פֶּסַח מַצָּה וּמָרוֹר. Some say that if one does not say פֶּסַח מַצָּה וּמָרוֹר, he has not fulfilled those three mitzvos properly (*Rashbam* and *Ramban*). However, others understand that not reciting פֶּסַח מַצָּה וּמָרוֹר means only that one has not fulfilled his obligation of *sippur Yetzias Mitzrayim*, but it does not affect his fulfilment of those three mitzvos themselves (*Rambam* and *Me'iri*). One practical difference between these two opinions is in a case where one is conducting a Seder and does not have any of these mitzvah items. According to the first opinion, there would be no reason to say פֶּסַח מַצָּה וּמָרוֹר, since one is not planning on performing these mitzvos. If, however, one needs to say פֶּסַח מַצָּה וּמָרוֹר to fulfill *sippur Yetzias Mitzrayim*, one is still required to say it (*Vayaged Moshe*).

When are you supposed to look at something that is on the קְעָרָה?

When one says פֶּסַח שֶׁהָיוּ אֲבוֹתֵינוּ אוֹכְלִים, he does not pick up the meat (as it might give the impression that he is sanctifying it as a *korban* outside the Beis HaMikdash, which is not allowed), but he should look

The matzah is raised and shown to the participants of the Seder.

מַצָּה זוֹ שֶׁאָנוּ אוֹכְלִים עַל שׁוּם מָה. עַל שׁוּם שֶׁלֹּא
הִסְפִּיק בְּצֵקָם שֶׁל אֲבוֹתֵינוּ לְהַחֲמִיץ, עַד שֶׁנִּגְלָה
עֲלֵיהֶם מֶלֶךְ מַלְכֵי הַמְּלָכִים הַקָּדוֹשׁ בָּרוּךְ הוּא וּגְאָלָם,
שֶׁנֶּאֱמַר, וַיֹּאפוּ אֶת הַבָּצֵק אֲשֶׁר הוֹצִיאוּ מִמִּצְרַיִם
עֻגֹת מַצּוֹת כִּי לֹא חָמֵץ, כִּי גֹרְשׁוּ מִמִּצְרַיִם וְלֹא יָכְלוּ
לְהִתְמַהְמֵהַּ וְגַם צֵדָה לֹא עָשׂוּ לָהֶם:

at it (*Bach* 473 and *Chok Yaakov* 473:36, brought in *Be'er Heitev* 473:25 but not mentioned in the *Mishnah Berurah*, see there 473:72).

What is done at the Seder to remember that the Korban Pesach was eaten בְּחִפָּזוֹן, in haste?

Rashi in *Berachos* (41a) writes that one is able to consume his food more speedily when he is reclining. Therefore, *Chazal* instituted reclining while we eat as a way of remembering that the Jews ate the *Korban Pesach* with alacrity, as it says וַאֲכַלְתֶּם אֹתוֹ בְּחִפָּזוֹן, *you shall eat it in haste* (12:11) (*Imrei Emes*, quoted in *Likkutei Yehudah, Parashas Bo*).

What is done at the Seder to commemorate the blood of the Korban Pesach that was placed on the two doorposts and the lintel of the house?

The two times we dip our food (one for *karpas* and one for *maror*) parallel the placing of the blood on the doorposts and the lintel (*Da'as Zekeinim* 12:8).

What was the symbolism of placing the blood on the two doorposts and the lintel of the house?

These three locations of blood corresponded to Avraham, Yitzchak, and Yaakov (*Ritva*).

The matzah is raised and shown to the participants of the Seder.

THIS *matzah that we eat—what does it represent? It represents the fact that the dough of our ancestors did not have a chance to become leavened before the King of kings, the Holy One, Blessed is He, appeared to them and redeemed them, as it says: "And they baked the dough that they had brought out of Egypt into unleavened cakes, for it had not become leavened; for they were driven out of Egypt and were unable to delay, nor had they prepared any food for themselves" (ibid. 12:39).*

What do the bread of poverty and the bread of redemption have in common?

They were both baked in a hurry. The Seforno (*Devarim* 16:3) explains that the Jewish people ate matzah in Mitzrayim (לֶחֶם עֹנִי, *the bread of poverty*) as they were always rushed by their Egyptian taskmasters, so their dough never had time to rise. Since they lived under these conditions, they merited to also be redeemed in a haste that did not allow their dough time to rise. This demonstrates that Hashem turned their suffering into freedom (וְהָפַכְתִּי אֶבְלָם לְשָׂשׂוֹן—*Yirmiyahu* 31:12). Thus, the matzos they ate in Mitzrayim and the matzos they baked when they left Mitzrayim are connected, as they were both eaten בְּחִפָּזוֹן, *in haste*.

The mitzvah of maror is only a Torah obligation when one eats it with the *Korban Pesach*. Why did the Rabbis institute that we must still eat *maror* today, when we don't have the *Korban Pesach*?

As a *zecher l'Mikdash*—to remember what it was like when the Beis HaMikdash was standing (*Shulchan Aruch HaRav* 475:6).

On the night of Rosh Hashanah, we eat symbolic foods with names that connote good things. This is

The maror is raised and shown to the participants of the Seder.

מָרוֹר זֶה שֶׁאָנוּ אוֹכְלִים עַל שׁוּם מָה. עַל שׁוּם שֶׁמֵּרְרוּ
הַמִּצְרִים אֶת חַיֵּי אֲבוֹתֵינוּ בְּמִצְרָיִם, שֶׁנֶּאֱמַר, וַיְמָרֲרוּ
אֶת חַיֵּיהֶם בַּעֲבֹדָה קָשָׁה בְּחֹמֶר וּבִלְבֵנִים וּבְכָל עֲבֹדָה
בַּשָּׂדֶה, אֵת כָּל עֲבֹדָתָם אֲשֶׁר עָבְדוּ בָהֶם בְּפָרֶךְ:

בְּכָל דּוֹר וָדוֹר חַיָּב אָדָם לִרְאוֹת אֶת עַצְמוֹ כְּאִלּוּ
הוּא יָצָא מִמִּצְרָיִם. שֶׁנֶּאֱמַר, וְהִגַּדְתָּ לְבִנְךָ בַּיּוֹם הַהוּא
לֵאמֹר בַּעֲבוּר זֶה עָשָׂה יְהֹוָה לִי בְּצֵאתִי מִמִּצְרָיִם. לֹא
אֶת אֲבוֹתֵינוּ בִּלְבַד גָּאַל הַקָּדוֹשׁ בָּרוּךְ הוּא, אֶלָּא אַף
אוֹתָנוּ גָּאַל עִמָּהֶם. שֶׁנֶּאֱמַר, וְאוֹתָנוּ הוֹצִיא מִשָּׁם,
לְמַעַן הָבִיא אוֹתָנוּ לָתֶת לָנוּ אֶת הָאָרֶץ אֲשֶׁר נִשְׁבַּע
לַאֲבוֹתֵינוּ:

known as סִימָנָא מִילְתָא, symbolic omens. Where at the Seder do we find the principle of סִימָנָא מִילְתָא?

The *Shulchan Aruch* (473:5) rules that one should try to use חֲזֶרֶת, romaine lettuce, for *maror* when possible. This applies even if it is more expensive than other types of *maror* (*Shulchan Aruch HaRav* 473:30). The reason seems to be that since the Hebrew word for romaine lettuce is חַסָּה, eating this form of *maror* can be symbolic of Hashem's mercy on us—חָס רַחֲמָנָא עֲלָן (*Levush* 473:5).

In every generation we must feel as if we ourselves left Mitzrayim. We also know that every person is obligated to say בִּשְׁבִילִי נִבְרָא הָעוֹלָם, the world was created for me (Sanhedrin 37a). What do you get if you put these two statements together?

The whole *Yetzias Mitzrayim* happened because of me! If one would

The maror is raised and shown to the participants of the Seder.

THIS *maror that we eat—what does it represent? It represents the fact that the Egyptians embittered the lives of our ancestors in Egypt, as it says: "And they embittered their lives with hard labor, with mortar and bricks, and with all sorts of work in the field; all their work with which they enslaved them with backbreaking labor" (ibid. 1:14).*

IN *each and every generation a person is obligated to regard himself as if he himself had left Egypt, as it says, "You shall tell your son on that day: 'Because of this Hashem did for me when I left Egypt'" (Shemos 13:8). It was not only our ancestors that the Holy One, Blessed is He, redeemed from Egypt; rather, He redeemed us with them as well, as it is says, "He brought us out from there, in order to bring us [here] to give us the land that He swore to our forefathers" (Devarim 6:21–3).*

internalize this concept and understand that *Yetzias Mitzrayim* happened *in order for me to receive the Torah*, he would apply himself to properly keep the Torah (*Netziv* on the Haggadah).

Where in the Haggadah is בְּכָל דּוֹר וָדוֹר חַיָּיב אָדָם לִרְאוֹת אֶת עַצְמוֹ supposed to be said, according to the oldest Haggadah in existence today?

In עֲבָדִים הָיִינוּ we say, *If Hashem would not have taken our forefathers out of Mitzrayim, then we and our children and grandchildren would all be enslaved to Pharaoh in Mitzrayim.* Rav Saadya Gaon's Haggadah (the earliest known Haggadah) then adds the logical continuation: since we would still be slaves to Pharaoh if Hashem would not have taken us out, therefore, *in every generation one has to view himself as if he himself left Mitzrayim.* (As to why our Haggadah does not follow this order, see *Ma'aseh Nissim* and other *mefarshim*.)

The matzah is covered and the cup of wine is raised while reciting the following paragraph. (Some have the custom to continue to raise the cup until it is drunk, after the blessing גאל ישראל.)

לְפִיכָךְ אֲנַחְנוּ חַיָּבִים לְהוֹדוֹת לְהַלֵּל לְשַׁבֵּחַ לְפָאֵר לְרוֹמֵם לְהַדֵּר לְבָרֵךְ לְעַלֵּה וּלְקַלֵּס לְמִי שֶׁעָשָׂה לַאֲבוֹתֵינוּ וְלָנוּ אֶת כָּל הַנִּסִּים הָאֵלֶּה. הוֹצִיאָנוּ מֵעַבְדוּת לְחֵרוּת, מִיָּגוֹן לְשִׂמְחָה, מֵאֵבֶל לְיוֹם טוֹב, וּמֵאֲפֵלָה לְאוֹר גָּדוֹל, וּמִשִּׁעְבּוּד לִגְאֻלָּה, וְנֹאמַר לְפָנָיו שִׁירָה חֲדָשָׁה הַלְלוּיָהּ:

לְמִי שֶׁעָשָׂה לַאֲבוֹתֵינוּ וְלָנוּ אֶת כָּל הַנִּסִּים הָאֵלּוּ, **to the One who did all these miracles to our forefathers and to us. Why don't we simply say "to Hashem"?**

The main goal of the miracles of *Yetzias Mitzrayim* is that one should discover Hashem in his daily, natural life (טֶבַע). Therefore, we refer to Hashem in an indirect way, to allude to the fact that we have to strive to discover Hashem in our own lives as well, even when He may seem hidden (Rav Yerucham Levovitz). Also, the style of the Haggadah is in a question and answer format. Therefore, when one says *"to the One who made all these miracles,"* one thinks to himself, "Who is that?"—and he answers to himself that it is Hashem who made all these miracles, thus fulfilling the goal of keeping to the question and answer style (*Pachad Yitzchak, Pesach 5*).

What item did the Jewish people get to wear only after they were redeemed from slavery?

We say in לְפִיכָךְ אֲנַחְנוּ חַיָּבִים לְהוֹדוֹת that Hashem took us out מֵאֵבֶל לְיוֹם טוֹב, *from mourning to a joyous day*. A mourner does not wear shoes, and neither did the Jewish people when they worked as slaves in Mitzrayim. It was therefore a big *simchah* to be allowed to wear shoes again (*Rashbatz*).

THEREFORE, *we are obligated to thank, to praise, to laud, to glorify, to exalt, to honor, to bless, to elevate, and to extol the One who performed all these miracles for our ancestors—and for us. He took us out from slavery to freedom, from sadness to joy, from mourning to festivity, from darkness to great light, and from subjugation to redemption. Now let us recite before Him a new song—Halleluyah!*

We say in לְפִיכָךְ אֲנַחְנוּ חַיָּבִים לְהוֹדוֹת that Hashem took us out מֵאֵבֶל לְיוֹם טוֹב, from mourning to a joyous day. But יוֹם טוֹב can also be translated as a festival. Which one is it?

Either it refers to the *yom tov* of Pesach—that instead of having seven days of *aveilus* for their children who were thrown into the Nile, *Klal Yisrael* now got to keep seven days of Pesach, or to the *yom tov* of Yom Kippur—that instead of *aveilus* over the sin of the Golden Calf, Hashem gave us a *yom tov* upon which he forgave us for that *aveirah* and gave us the second set of *luchos* (*Otzros HaHaggadah*, p. 609).

Which parts of *Hallel* were composed when the Jews left Mitzrayim?

The *nevi'im* in Mitzrayim composed parts of *Hallel* from לֹא לָנוּ until the end. It was only later, when the Jewish people actually left Mitzrayim, that they composed the first two *perakim* of *Hallel*—הַלְלוּ עַבְדֵי ה' and בְּצֵאת יִשְׂרָאֵל מִמִּצְרַיִם. Therefore, before we begin the *seudah* we say the parts of *Hallel* that were added at *Yetzias Mitzrayim*, and we finish with the *berachah* of אֲשֶׁר גְּאָלָנוּ. Only afterward do we say the rest of *Hallel* (*Pesach Doros*).

הַלְלוּיָהּ, הַלְלוּ עַבְדֵי יהוה, הַלְלוּ אֶת שֵׁם יהוה: יְהִי שֵׁם יהוה מְבֹרָךְ, מֵעַתָּה וְעַד עוֹלָם: מִמִּזְרַח שֶׁמֶשׁ עַד מְבוֹאוֹ, מְהֻלָּל שֵׁם יהוה: רָם עַל כָּל גּוֹיִם יהוה, עַל הַשָּׁמַיִם כְּבוֹדוֹ: מִי כַּיהוה אֱלֹהֵינוּ, הַמַּגְבִּיהִי לָשָׁבֶת: הַמַּשְׁפִּילִי לִרְאוֹת, בַּשָּׁמַיִם וּבָאָרֶץ: מְקִימִי מֵעָפָר דָּל, מֵאַשְׁפֹּת יָרִים אֶבְיוֹן: לְהוֹשִׁיבִי עִם נְדִיבִים, עִם נְדִיבֵי עַמּוֹ: מוֹשִׁיבִי עֲקֶרֶת הַבַּיִת, אֵם הַבָּנִים שְׂמֵחָה, הַלְלוּיָהּ: בְּצֵאת יִשְׂרָאֵל מִמִּצְרָיִם, בֵּית יַעֲקֹב מֵעַם לֹעֵז: הָיְתָה יְהוּדָה לְקָדְשׁוֹ יִשְׂרָאֵל מַמְשְׁלוֹתָיו: הַיָּם רָאָה וַיָּנֹס, הַיַּרְדֵּן יִסֹּב לְאָחוֹר: הֶהָרִים רָקְדוּ כְאֵילִים, גְּבָעוֹת כִּבְנֵי צֹאן: מַה לְּךָ הַיָּם כִּי תָנוּס, הַיַּרְדֵּן תִּסֹּב לְאָחוֹר: הֶהָרִים תִּרְקְדוּ כְאֵילִים, גְּבָעוֹת כִּבְנֵי צֹאן: מִלִּפְנֵי אָדוֹן חוּלִי אָרֶץ מִלִּפְנֵי אֱלוֹהַּ יַעֲקֹב: הַהֹפְכִי הַצּוּר אֲגַם מָיִם, חַלָּמִישׁ לְמַעְיְנוֹ מָיִם:

Where in the first perek of Hallel is there an allusion to the fact that the Egyptians experienced fifty makkos at the Yam Suf?

In the first perek of Hallel, we find that the letter yud appears five times, at the ends of the words הַמַּגְבִּיהִי, הַמַּשְׁפִּילִי, מְקִימִי, לְהוֹשִׁיבִי, מוֹשִׁיבִי, and it seems superfluous. The gematria of yud is ten, and this alludes to the five times ten makkos (fifty in total) that the Egyptians received at the Yam Suf (Rokeach).

How many times do we say שֶׁהֶחֱיָנוּ on Seder night?

In the berachah of וְהִגִּיעָנוּ הַלַּיְלָה הַזֶּה לֶאֱכָל בּוֹ מַצָּה וּמָרוֹר אֲשֶׁר גְּאָלָנוּ we say, and You have made us reach this night to eat matzah and maror. The Rokeach (371) writes that saying this is the equivalent of saying שֶׁהֶחֱיָנוּ. So we

(Psalm 113)

HALLELUYAH! *Praise, you servants of Hashem, praise the Name of Hashem! May Hashem's Name be blessed from now to eternity. From the place of the rising of the sun to the place of its setting Hashem's Name is praised. Hashem is raised above all nations, His glory is over the heavens. Who is like Hashem our God, Who dwells on high, and lowers Himself to look upon heaven and earth! He raises up the poor from the dust, He lifts the needy from the trash heaps—to seat them with nobles, with the nobles of His people. He causes the barren woman to be established with a family, a joyful mother of children. Halleluyah!*

(Psalm 114)

WHEN *Israel went out of Egypt, the House of Yaakov from a people of a foreign language, Yehudah became His sanctifier, Israel His dominions. The sea saw and fled, the Jordan turned back. The mountains skipped like rams, the hills like young sheep. What is with you, O sea, that you flee, O Jordan, that you turn back? You mountains, why do you skip like rams; you hills, like young sheep? Tremble, O earth, from before Hashem, from before the God of Yaakov, Who transforms a rock into a pool of water, a hard stone into a spring of water!*

say שֶׁהֶחֱיָנוּ twice: once during Kiddush for the *yom tov* of Pesach, and a second time at this point for the mitzvah of matzah and *maror*.

Ashkenazim make a separate *berachah* on each of the four cups (Rama 474:1). When would one **not** make a *berachah* on the second cup, even according to the Rama?

1. If one intended to include the second cup in his *berachah* over the first cup (*Pri Megadim* 474:1).

2. When making the *berachah* over *chamar medinah* [a drink that is commonly served when entertaining important company].

The cup of wine is held in the hand as the following paragraph is recited:

בָּרוּךְ אַתָּה יהוה אֱלֹהֵינוּ מֶלֶךְ הָעוֹלָם, אֲשֶׁר גְּאָלֵנוּ וְגָאַל
אֶת אֲבוֹתֵינוּ מִמִּצְרַיִם, וְהִגִּיעֵנוּ הַלַּיְלָה הַזֶּה לֶאֱכָל בּוֹ מַצָּה
וּמָרוֹר. כֵּן יהוה אֱלֹהֵינוּ וֵאלֹהֵי אֲבוֹתֵינוּ יַגִּיעֵנוּ לְמוֹעֲדִים
וְלִרְגָלִים אֲחֵרִים הַבָּאִים לִקְרָאתֵנוּ לְשָׁלוֹם, שְׂמֵחִים בְּבִנְיַן
עִירֶךָ, וְשָׂשִׂים בַּעֲבוֹדָתֶךָ, וְנֹאכַל שָׁם מִן הַזְּבָחִים וּמִן הַפְּסָחִים
אֲשֶׁר יַגִּיעַ דָּמָם עַל קִיר מִזְבַּחֲךָ לְרָצוֹן וְנוֹדֶה לְךָ שִׁיר חָדָשׁ
עַל גְּאֻלָּתֵנוּ וְעַל פְּדוּת נַפְשֵׁנוּ: בָּרוּךְ אַתָּה יהוה גָּאַל יִשְׂרָאֵל:

בָּרוּךְ אַתָּה יהוה אֱלֹהֵינוּ מֶלֶךְ הָעוֹלָם,
בּוֹרֵא פְּרִי הַגָּפֶן:

The wine is now drunk, while reclining on the left side.

רחצה

Since it is forbidden to interrupt unnecessarily between the washing of the hands and the eating of the Korech sandwich, the leader should relate to the participants the various rules of matzah consumption before washing his hands. He should remind everyone that they must eat a kezayis of matzah within a time span of כדי אכילת פרס (two minutes according to the most stringent opinion; four or even nine minutes according to more lenient opinions) and that the matzah and Korech must be eaten while reclining on the left side.

The hands are washed in preparation for the meal and the following blessing is said:

בָּרוּךְ אַתָּה יהוה אֱלֹהֵינוּ מֶלֶךְ הָעוֹלָם, אֲשֶׁר
קִדְּשָׁנוּ בְּמִצְוֹתָיו, וְצִוָּנוּ עַל נְטִילַת יָדָיִם:

Why? Even though *chamar medinah* is acceptable where one does not have wine (*Rama* 483:1), since some *Rishonim* hold that one cannot be *yotzei* with *chamar medinah*, one does not make a

The cup of wine is held in the hand as the following paragraph is recited:

BLESSED *are You, Hashem, our God, King of the universe, Who has redeemed us and redeemed our ancestors from Egypt, and allowed us to reach this night, to eat matzah and maror on it. So too, Hashem, our God and the God of our fathers, allow us to reach in peace other holidays and festivals in the future, happy in the rebuilding of Your city, and joyful in Your Temple service. And there we will partake of sacrifices and Pesach offerings, whose blood will be poured on the wall of Your altar for Your acceptance, and we will give thanks to You with a new song over our redemption and the salvation of our souls. Blessed are You, Hashem, Who redeemed Israel.*

Blessed are You, Hashem, our God, King of the universe, Who creates the fruit of the vine.

The wine is now drunk, while reclining on the left side.

RACHTZAH

Since it is forbidden to interrupt unnecessarily between the washing of the hands and the eating of the Korech sandwich, the leader should relate to the participants the various rules of matzah consumption before washing his hands. He should remind everyone that they must eat a kezayis of matzah within a time span of כדי אכילת פרס (two minutes according to the most stringent opinion; four or even nine minutes according to more lenient opinions) and that the matzah and Korech must be eaten while reclining on the left side.

The hands are washed in preparation for the meal and the following blessing is said:

Blessed are You, Hashem, our God, King of the universe, Who has sanctified us through His commandments, and commanded us concerning the washing of the hands.

berachah on each of the four cups. In such a case, it is preferable to do as the *Shulchan Aruch* suggests (474:1) and only make a *berachah* on the first and third cups (*Sha'ar HaTziyun* 483:8).

מוֹצִיא

The three matzos are held and the following blessing is said:

בָּרוּךְ אַתָּה יהוה אֱלֹהֵינוּ מֶלֶךְ הָעוֹלָם,
הַמּוֹצִיא לֶחֶם מִן הָאָרֶץ:

מַצָּה

The bottom matzah is released. While the top two matzos are held, the following blessing is said:

בָּרוּךְ אַתָּה יהוה אֱלֹהֵינוּ מֶלֶךְ הָעוֹלָם, אֲשֶׁר
קִדְּשָׁנוּ בְּמִצְוֹתָיו, וְצִוָּנוּ עַל אֲכִילַת מַצָּה:

A kezayis from each of the two matzos is eaten, while reclining on the left side.

מָרוֹר

*A kezayis of maror is dipped in charoses. The charoses should then be shaken off the maror
(so as not to sweeten its bitter taste) and the following blessing is said:*

בָּרוּךְ אַתָּה יהוה אֱלֹהֵינוּ מֶלֶךְ הָעוֹלָם, אֲשֶׁר
קִדְּשָׁנוּ בְּמִצְוֹתָיו, וְצִוָּנוּ עַל אֲכִילַת מָרוֹר:

The kezayis of maror is eaten (without reclining).

When should one eat matzah before saying the Haggadah?

If one did not start the Seder at the beginning of the night and
the time is approaching חֲצוֹת (midnight), it is preferable to eat the
matzah before saying the Haggadah. This is because many *Rishonim*
hold that one does not fulfill the mitzvah of matzah if he eats it after
חֲצוֹת. In such a scenario, the correct procedure would be: Kiddush,
matzah, and *maror*, Haggadah, and then eat the meal (*Mishnah
Berurah* 477:6).

MOTZI

The three matzos are held and the following blessing is said:

Blessed are You, Hashem, our God, King of the universe, Who brings forth bread from the earth.

MATZAH

The bottom matzah is released. While the top two matzos are held, the following blessing is said:

Blessed are You, Hashem, our God, King of the universe, Who has sanctified us through His commandments, and commanded us concerning the eating of matzah.

A kezayis from each of the two matzos is eaten, while reclining on the left side.

MAROR

A kezayis of maror is dipped in charoses. The charoses should then be shaken off the maror (so as not to sweeten its bitter taste) and the following blessing is said:

Blessed are You, Hashem, our God, King of the universe, Who has sanctified us through His commandments, and commanded us concerning the eating of maror.

The kezayis of maror is eaten (without reclining).

What would the Chasam Sofer do with the leftover maror from the Seder nights?

He would eat it at the meal of the second day of *yom tov* since they are שְׁיָרֵי מִצְוָה, remains of a mitzvah, and should therefore not be discarded in a disrespectful manner (*Minhagei Chasam Sofer* 10:18).

כּוֹרֵךְ

A kezayis of the bottom matzah is taken together with a kezayis of maror (some people dip the maror in charoses), and the following is said:

זֵכֶר לְמִקְדָּשׁ כְּהִלֵּל.

כֵּן עָשָׂה הִלֵּל, בִּזְמַן שֶׁבֵּית הַמִּקְדָּשׁ הָיָה קַיָּם, הָיָה כּוֹרֵךְ (פֶּסַח) מַצָּה וּמָרוֹר וְאוֹכֵל בְּיַחַד, לְקַיֵּם מַה שֶׁנֶּאֱמַר, עַל מַצּוֹת וּמְרֹרִים יֹאכְלֻהוּ:

The matzah-and-maror combination is eaten, while reclining on the left side.

What is the connection between בִּרְכַּת יוֹצֵר אוֹר and maror?

In בִּרְכַּת יוֹצֵר אוֹר we say תָּמִיד מְסַפְּרִים כְּבוֹד אֵ-ל, and the *roshei teivos* (first letter of each word) spell out תַּמְכָא, which is horseradish, one of the ingredients that can be used for *maror* (*Shu"t Chasam Sofer, Orach Chaim* 132).

What can prevent one's stomach from becoming bloated from eating vegetables?

Dipping vegetables into *charoses*! The Gemara (*Pesachim* 114a) brings the opinion of the *Chachamim* who hold that there is no intrinsic mitzvah in dipping the *maror* into *charoses*. It is only done to negate the *kappa*. This *kappa* is usually translated as poison (*Rashbam* 115b) [see *Tiferes Yisroel* to *Pesachim* 10:3, who explains that this refers to the sharp taste of the *maror*, which can be harmful to the body] or small worms (*Rabbeinu Channanel* 115a).

Rav Hai Gaon (quoted by Abudraham) explains that *kappa* is the feeling of air in the stomach that certain foods can cause. Dipping the food into *charoses* serves to contravene this inflation of air in one's stomach.

KORECH

A kezayis of the bottom matzah is taken together with a kezayis of maror (some people dip the maror in charoses), and the following is said:

IN *remembrance of the Temple, like Hillel. This is what Hillel did, when the Temple was still standing. He would combine matzah and maror and eat them together, in fulfillment of what it says: "They shall eat it together with matzos and maror" (Bamidbar 9:11).*

The matzah-and-maror combination is eaten, while reclining on the left side.

People fight over me, and I am a fighter too. What am I?

Charoses! The *Yerushalmi* (*Pesachim* 10:3) says that the name of the mixture we dip the *maror* into is called רוֹבֶה. The *Korban Ha'Edah* (ibid.) explains that it got this name, which indicates רִיב (fighting), since the Rabbis fought over it: Rav Elazar bar Tzadok said *charoses* is a mitzvah, while the *Chachamim* said it is not a mitzvah (Mishnah in *Pesachim* 114a). The *Gilyon Efraim* (ibid.), on the other hand, says that the name represents how *charoses* fights against the *kappa* (poison, worms, or inflated air) and negates it.

What is the connection between the berachah we make on maror and the berachah we recite before shaking the lulav on Sukkos?

The *berachah* we recite on the four species is עַל נְטִילַת לוּלָב, and the esrog, *hadasim*, and *aravos* are all included in the *berachah* on the lulav. Likewise, the *charoses* is included in the *berachah* of the *maror* and therefore does not require a separate *berachah* (Rabbeinu Manoach, *Chametz U'Matzah* 7:11).

First you hang me up, and then you chop me. What am I?

Some have a *minhag* to use the fruits that hung in the sukkah for the *charoses*, applying the principle of *since one mitzvah was done*

שלחן עורך

It is customary to eat eggs at the beginning of the meal. Care should be taken to leave enough time in order to be able to eat the afikoman before halachic midnight. One should also be sure to leave some appetite for the afikoman.

with it, we should do another mitzvah with it, (*Vayaged Moshe* 4:3 from *Berachos* 39b).

Why can charoses conceivably be made of mud?

Some would put a bit of actual mud or bits of grated bricks into their *charoses* to represent the hard work the Jewish people engaged in during their slavery in Egypt (see *Shibolei HaLeket* 218). However, the *Birkei Yosef* quotes Maharam di Lunzano, who strongly argues against this *minhag* and calls it a ridiculous and bizarre custom. Would you take blood out of someone on Purim to remember the evil decree of Haman? Likewise, you should not put any real pieces of mud or bricks into the *charoses* (see further in *Birkei Yosef* 473:12, where he attributes this custom to a spelling mistake in the words of the Rashbam 116a, s.v. "tavlin").

Charoses should ideally taste sharp but also sweet (see *Pesachim* 115b and 116a). Which charoses ingredient fits both of these descriptions?

The Rashbam (115b) explains that the sweet taste of *charoses* comes from the apples, and he also says (116a) that apples cause it to have a sharp taste.

When does a piece of matzah (besides for the afikoman) represent the Korban Pesach?

Hillel would eat פֶּסַח מַצָּה וּמָרוֹר together (opinion of Rashbam 115a, s.v. "shehaya"). As a *zecher* to this, many have the *minhag* to break the matzah for *Korech* into two pieces and put the *maror* in between the two pieces. This is done to represent the three things Hillel would eat

SHULCHAN ORECH

It is customary to eat eggs at the beginning of the meal. Care should be taken to leave enough time in order to be able to eat the afikoman before halachic midnight. One should also be sure to leave some appetite for the afikoman.

together: *Pesach* (one layer of matzah), matzah (the second layer of matzah), and *maror* (in the middle) (*Vayaged Moshe* 26:7).

When does an entire matzah represent maror?

The three matzos at the Seder represent the three items Hillel would use: פֶּסַח מַצָּה וּמְרוֹר. Thus, the middle matzah represents *maror* (*Pri Etz Chayim, Sha'ar Chag HaMatzos*).

The maror for Korech should be dipped into charoses (Mishnah Berurah 475:19). Some authorities disagree. Why?

The Rama brings the opinion (475:1) that one should not dip the *Korech* sandwich into *charoses*. One reason given is that it would constitute a third dipping, and, as we say in מַה נִּשְׁתַּנָּה, *Chazal* only instituted two dippings, not three (*Ra'aviyah* 2:525, see also *Taz* 475:6).

If one does not dip the maror of his Korech sandwich into charoses, how does he negate the harmful effects of the kappa (poison, worm, or inflation of air)?

We have seen earlier that one needs to dip the *maror* into *charoses* to negate the harmful effects of the *kappa*. If one does not dip the *maror* from *Korech* into *charoses*, he still has other options: He can eat hot matzos (*Kaf HaChaim* 458:12) or drink hot water afterward (*Hilchesa Gevirta* 46). This is based on the Gemara (*Pesachim* 116a) that says hot food and drinks also negate the potentially harmful effects of the *kappa*. As was mentioned before, the *Mishnah Berurah* 475:19 rules that one *should* dip the *maror* of the *Korech* sandwich into *charoses*.

צָפוּן

At the end of the meal, a kezayis (according to some, two kezaysim) of the matzah that had earlier been hidden away is eaten as the afikoman. The afikoman should be eaten while reclining on the left side.

One may not eat anything after the afikoman, nor may he drink anything (besides the third and fourth cups of wine) other than water.

We are supposed to eat matzah because it is a mitzvah and not just because we like the taste. How do we show that?

One reason behind eating matzah and *maror* together for *Korech* is to teach us an important lesson: Just like one does not eat the bitter herbs for their taste, but only לְשֵׁם שָׁמַיִם (for the sake of the mitzvah), so too one should eat matzah לְשֵׁם שָׁמַיִם and not just on account of its taste (*Yitav Panim, Shabbos HaGadol 26*).

How does *Korech* demonstrate unity of the Jewish people?

The *Korban Pesach* has a taste and a smell (symbolizing the people who possess both Torah and *ma'asim tovim*), matzah has a taste but no smell (symbolizing people who only possess Torah and not *ma'asim tovim*), and *maror* has no [good] taste or smell (symbolizing individuals devoid of Torah and *ma'asim tovim*). Hillel would show the *achdus* of the Jewish nation by combining these three types together (*Birkas HaShir*).

Who used to eat eggs on the night of the fifteenth of Nissan before the Exodus happened?

In Mitzrayim, the Jewish people used to get together every year and mourn their slavery by eating eggs, the traditional symbol of mourning. They would gather together on the fifteenth of Nissan, the night that their slavery was decreed at the בְּרִית בֵּין הַבְּתָרִים—the covenant formed between Hashem and Avraham Avinu—and grieve over their sorry state. To remember this, we eat eggs at our Seder as well (Chasam Sofer). We can imagine how, similarly, we will one day eat eggs at our festive Tishah

TZAFUN

At the end of the meal, a kezayis (according to some, two kezeisim) of the matzah that had earlier been hidden away is eaten as the afikoman. The afikoman should be eaten while reclining on the left side.

One may not eat anything after the afikoman, nor may he drink anything (besides the third and fourth cups of wine) other than water.

b'Av meal, commemorating that the day was once one of mourning, when we ate eggs to symbolize our pain over the loss of the Beis HaMikdash.

Why did the author of the *Chayei Adam* (Rav Avraham Danzig, 1748–1821) not eat eggs at the Seder (although the minhag to eat them is brought down by the *Rama* 476:2)?

The *Chayei Adam* writes that if eating eggs will make a person too full to eat the *afikoman* (to the point that eating it would be considered אֲכִילָה גַּסָה, gorging), he should rather not eat the eggs and save his appetite for the *afikoman*. The *Chayei Adam* (130:12) writes that he himself did not eat the eggs for this very reason (the *Mishnah Berurah* quotes part of this *Chayei Adam* in 476:13).

What should one be careful with when he eats the eggs, according to the *Kaf HaChaim*?

The *Kaf HaChaim* (476:24) writes that one should not verbally express that he is eating the eggs as a sign of mourning. Although the *Rama* mentions (476:2) that we eat eggs at the Seder as a sign of mourning over the fact that we do not have a Beis HaMikdash, verbalizing this violates the prohibition of דַּרְכֵי הָאֱמוֹרִי, following the ancient pagan practices of superstition. It is unclear why verbally mentioning the reason for eating the eggs should pose a problem of דַּרְכֵי הָאֱמוֹרִי (Rav Yitzchok Zilberstein, *shlita*, in a written response to this author).

What type of roasted meat can never be eaten at the Seder?

The *Shulchan Aruch* (476:1) writes that eating roasted meat on the

night of the Seder depends on the *minhag* of the particular place one is in; some *minhagim* allow it, while others do not (the *Mishnah Berurah* 476:1 explains that our custom is to be stringent and not eat roasted meat at all during the Seder). However, even in a place where the custom is to allow eating roasted meat, eating a *gedi mekulas* (a lamb that has been roasted completely in one piece) at the Seder is never permitted, as it would appear as though one is eating a *Korban Pesach* outside the Beis HaMikdash, which is not allowed (*Shulchan Aruch* 476:1). According to this opinion, one **would** be allowed to eat a calf that has been roasted in one piece (*Mishnah Berurah* 476:10). Also, even where the *minhag* is to allow eating roasted meat, one may not eat the *zero'a* that is on the קְעָרָה. The *zero'a* represents the *Korban Pesach*, and eating it would appear as though one is eating the *Korban Pesach*, which is not allowed (*Shulchan Aruch HaRav* 476:21).

When would all agree that it was allowed to have roasted meat at the Seder?

We do not eat roasted meat on Seder night [according to the accepted custom mentioned above], as it would appear as though we were eating the *Korban Pesach* outside of Yerushalayim (*Rashi* to *Pesachim* 53a). The *Pri Megadim* (476:1) writes that this *minhag* only developed after the destruction of the Beis HaMikdash. In the times of the Beis HaMikdash, one could eat roasted meat anywhere, as it was obvious that the *Korban Pesach* could not be brought outside of Yerushalayim. However, after the destruction of the Beis HaMikdash, if someone was seen eating what appeared to be the *Korban Pesach*, people could come to believe that one is allowed to bring a *Korban Pesach* out of Yerushalayim, and this could, Heaven forbid, lead people to commit the serious transgression of bringing a *korban* outside of Yerushalayim, which is liable for *kares*.

You are allowed to roast food for the Seder as long as it does not require _____?

Shechitah. Anything that does not require *shechitah* may be eaten roasted, such as eggs and fish (*Mishnah Berurah* 476:9, see also *Aruch HaShulchan* 476:4 for further study).

What do we eat at the Seder to show that we are not allowed to eat roasted meat?

The *Tur* (476) writes that it is a מִנְהָג כָּשֵׁר, a correct *minhag*, to eat boiled meat at the Seder. The *Beis Yosef* (476:2) explains that it is proper to do so, since in this way one is demonstrating that he is not allowed to eat roasted meat. If a person were not to eat any meat, it would not be clear that there is a specific problem with eating roasted meat.

When does meat that was intended for use at the Seder have to be buried?

The Gemara says in *Pesachim* (53a) that one is not allowed to say *"This meat is for Pesach,"* since it carries the implication that one is sanctifying the meat to eat it as a *korban* (which is not allowed when we don't have a Beis HaMikdash). According to the *Bach* (469), if one said *"This meat is for Pesach,"* the meat becomes forbidden, and one may not derive any benefit from it. It therefore must be buried or likewise disposed of to prevent anyone from coming into contact with it, just like other materials that one may not derive benefit from. The final halachah, however, is not like this. The *Mishnah Berurah* (469:1) rules that it is only forbidden to say *"This meat is for Pesach,"* but ex post facto the meat may still be eaten.

What do we eat at the Seder to remember the Korban Chagigah?

The *Shulchan Aruch* (477:1) writes that we eat one *kezayis* of matzah for the *afikoman*. The *Mishnah Berurah* (ibid.) writes that, ideally, one should eat two *kezeisim*. Why? According to the *Chayei Adam* (130:13), one *kezayis* corresponds to the *Korban Pesach*, and one *kezayis* corresponds to the *Korban Chagigah*. According to the Vilna Gaon (476:2), eating eggs during *Shulchan Orech* is also a *zecher* to the *Korban Chagigah*.

According to the Maharal, why do we eat the afikoman?

The *Rishonim* cite two basic reasons for eating the *afikoman*: (1) to remember the *Korban Pesach* (this opinion is codified in *Shulchan Aruch* 477) and (2) to remember the matzah that was eaten together with the *Korban Pesach* (therefore, one should ideally eat two *kezeisim* to

fulfill both opinions, *Mishnah Berurah* 477:1). The Maharal (*Gevuros Hashem* 63) takes a different approach. In his opinion, the reason we eat the *afikoman* is to allow the taste of matzah to linger in our mouths. Therefore, the halachah that prohibits eating after the *afikoman* is not merely a "secondary" halachah that applies to the *afikoman*, but is the very reason we eat it.

How can the prohibition against eating after the afikoman serve as a reminder to say Hallel?

In the times of the Beis HaMikdash, the *Korban Pesach* was often eaten in cramped conditions. After eating the *afikoman*, the participants would climb up to the roof, where they would recite *Hallel*. Since they were going from one place to another, there was a possibility that they might forget to say *Hallel*. The Rabbis therefore banned further eating after the *Korban Pesach*, and in this way people would be reminded to say *Hallel*. Although this reason is no longer applicable today, as we don't move from place to place during the Seder, we don't eat after the *afikoman* as a זֵכֶר לְמִקְדָּשׁ (*Ba'al HaMa'or Pesachim* 119b).

Why does the afikoman make me so tired?

The *Ra'avan* translates the word *afikoman* as *afik v'nim, go to sleep,* as following the *afikoman*, one must go to sleep without any further food intake. Obviously, though, he should not go to sleep before he has finished the second part of the Haggadah, which includes *Hallel* and the last two cups. (The *Shulchan Aruch* 481:2 cites the halachah that one should stay awake and speak about *Yetzias Mitzrayim* until sleep overtakes him.)

In the times of the Mishnah, what was the usual practice following dessert at a festive meal?

They would sing *zemiros*—but not at the Seder! *Afikoman* can be translated as *afiku minei*, which means "remove all types of songs." Seder night is not a time to sing post-dessert *zemiros* since there is a requirement to immediately say *Hallel* (*Yerushalmi Pesachim* 10:6 with *Korban Ha'Edah*).

Eating the afikoman can be a segulah to merit three gifts: children, health, and sustenance. How so?

For having children: the gematria of afikoman equals כֵּן יִרְבֶּה, so they multiplied (Shemos 1:12) (Imrei Noam 87). For health: afikoman is also the gematria of רוֹפֵא, doctor (Me'or VaShemesh) There are those who eat a small piece of the afikoman throughout the year whenever they feel pain (Likkutei Meir, Pesach 58). For parnasah: the first three letters of afikoman are the roshei teivos of פּוֹתֵחַ אֶת יָדֶךָ, You open your hand, and the afikoman is therefore seen as a segulah for parnasah (Me'or VaShemesh).

What would go into the Shabbos HaGadol cholent in the kehillah of Frankfurt?

The minhag in Frankfurt (brought in Otzros HaHaggadah, p. 700) was to save a piece of the afikoman all year and put it in the cholent on Shabbos HaGadol (provided that one would check the piece carefully to ensure that there was no insect infestation evident on the matzah). We can suggest that perhaps the rationale for doing so was to convey an important lesson: It is the emunah that we internalize on Pesach that propels us spiritually throughout the year. When next year's Shabbos HaGadol comes around, we have, so to speak, "used up" all the inspiration we gained last Pesach, and we symbolize this by throwing the afikoman from the previous year into the cholent. This is to remind us that this year's Seder should again serve to boost our emunah and give us chizuk for the coming year.

"Do not swallow anything else after taking this medicine so as not to hamper the medicine's absorption into the body." What does this mashal explain?

Why we don't eat anything after the afikoman. Eating the afikoman is considered a refuah for the neshamah—the Zohar calls the matzah "the bread of healing" (2:183b). Often, after taking a critical medicine, a patient is advised not to eat for a period of time to allow the medicine time to work. Likewise, the afikoman needs time to work on healing a person's neshamah, and therefore one cannot eat after the afikoman (Yitav Lev, Shemini).

בָּרֵךְ

The third cup of wine, over which Birkas HaMazon is recited, is poured. It is customary that the master of the house lead Birkas HaMazon at the Seder.

שִׁיר הַמַּעֲלוֹת, בְּשׁוּב יְהֹוָה אֶת שִׁיבַת צִיּוֹן הָיִינוּ כְּחֹלְמִים: אָז יִמָּלֵא שְׂחוֹק פִּינוּ וּלְשׁוֹנֵנוּ רִנָּה, אָז יֹאמְרוּ בַגּוֹיִם הִגְדִּיל יְהֹוָה לַעֲשׂוֹת עִם אֵלֶּה: הִגְדִּיל יְהֹוָה לַעֲשׂוֹת עִמָּנוּ הָיִינוּ שְׂמֵחִים: שׁוּבָה יְהֹוָה אֶת שְׁבִיתֵנוּ כַּאֲפִיקִים בַּנֶּגֶב: הַזֹּרְעִים בְּדִמְעָה בְּרִנָּה יִקְצֹרוּ: הָלוֹךְ יֵלֵךְ וּבָכֹה נֹשֵׂא מֶשֶׁךְ הַזָּרַע בֹּא יָבֹא בְרִנָּה נֹשֵׂא אֲלֻמֹּתָיו:

The following invitation to say Birkas HaMazon is added when there are three adult males present. When ten adult males are present, the words in parentheses are also added:

Leader

רַבּוֹתַי נְבָרֵךְ:

Others

יְהִי שֵׁם יהוה מְבֹרָךְ מֵעַתָּה וְעַד עוֹלָם:

Leader

יְהִי שֵׁם יהוה מְבֹרָךְ מֵעַתָּה וְעַד עוֹלָם:
בִּרְשׁוּת מָרָנָן וְרַבָּנָן וְרַבּוֹתַי, נְבָרֵךְ (אֱלֹהֵינוּ) שֶׁאָכַלְנוּ מִשֶּׁלּוֹ:

Others

בָּרוּךְ (אֱלֹהֵינוּ) שֶׁאָכַלְנוּ מִשֶּׁלּוֹ וּבְטוּבוֹ חָיִינוּ:

Leader

בָּרוּךְ (אֱלֹהֵינוּ) שֶׁאָכַלְנוּ מִשֶּׁלּוֹ וּבְטוּבוֹ חָיִינוּ:

BARECH

The third cup of wine, over which Birkas HaMazon is recited, is poured. It is customary that the master of the house lead Birkas HaMazon at the Seder.

(Psalm 126) A Song of Ascents. When Hashem will return the exiles of Zion, we will be like dreamers. Then our mouth will be filled with laughter, and our tongue with shouts of joy. Then will they say among the nations, "Hashem has done great things for these People." Hashem has done great things for us. Then we will be joyful. Hashem, return our exiles, like streams in parched land. Those who sow in tears will reap with shouts of joy. He keeps going along weeping, carrying the load of seed; but he will surely come back with shouts of joy, carrying his sheaves.

The following invitation to say Birkas HaMazon is added when there are three adult males present. When ten adult males are present, the words in parentheses are also added:

Leader

Gentlemen, let us bless!

Others

May the Name of Hashem be blessed from now to eternity.

Leader

May the Name of Hashem be blessed from now to eternity.

With the permission of my masters, teachers, and gentlemen—Let us bless Him (our God), of whose [bounty] we have eaten.

Others

Blessed be He (our God) of whose bounty we have eaten, and by Whose grace we live.

Leader

Blessed be He (our God) of whose bounty we have eaten, and by Whose grace we live.

בָּרוּךְ אַתָּה יהוה אֱלֹהֵינוּ מֶלֶךְ הָעוֹלָם, הַזָּן אֶת הָעוֹלָם
כֻּלּוֹ בְּטוּבוֹ בְּחֵן בְּחֶסֶד וּבְרַחֲמִים, הוּא נוֹתֵן לֶחֶם לְכָל
בָּשָׂר כִּי לְעוֹלָם חַסְדּוֹ, וּבְטוּבוֹ הַגָּדוֹל תָּמִיד לֹא חָסַר
לָנוּ וְאַל יֶחְסַר לָנוּ מָזוֹן לְעוֹלָם וָעֶד, בַּעֲבוּר שְׁמוֹ הַגָּדוֹל,
כִּי הוּא אֵל זָן וּמְפַרְנֵס לַכֹּל וּמֵטִיב לַכֹּל, וּמֵכִין מָזוֹן לְכָל
בְּרִיּוֹתָיו אֲשֶׁר בָּרָא. בָּרוּךְ אַתָּה יהוה, הַזָּן אֶת הַכֹּל:

נוֹדֶה לְךָ יהוה אֱלֹהֵינוּ עַל שֶׁהִנְחַלְתָּ לַאֲבוֹתֵינוּ, אֶרֶץ
חֶמְדָּה טוֹבָה וּרְחָבָה, וְעַל שֶׁהוֹצֵאתָנוּ יהוה אֱלֹהֵינוּ
מֵאֶרֶץ מִצְרַיִם, וּפְדִיתָנוּ מִבֵּית עֲבָדִים, וְעַל בְּרִיתְךָ
שֶׁחָתַמְתָּ בִּבְשָׂרֵנוּ, וְעַל תּוֹרָתְךָ שֶׁלִּמַּדְתָּנוּ, וְעַל חֻקֶּיךָ
שֶׁהוֹדַעְתָּנוּ, וְעַל חַיִּים חֵן וָחֶסֶד שֶׁחוֹנַנְתָּנוּ, וְעַל אֲכִילַת
מָזוֹן שָׁאַתָּה זָן וּמְפַרְנֵס אוֹתָנוּ תָּמִיד, בְּכָל יוֹם וּבְכָל
עֵת וּבְכָל שָׁעָה:

וְעַל הַכֹּל יהוה אֱלֹהֵינוּ אֲנַחְנוּ מוֹדִים לָךְ, וּמְבָרְכִים
אוֹתָךְ, יִתְבָּרַךְ שִׁמְךָ בְּפִי כָּל חַי תָּמִיד לְעוֹלָם וָעֶד.
כַּכָּתוּב, וְאָכַלְתָּ וְשָׂבָעְתָּ, וּבֵרַכְתָּ אֶת יהוה אֱלֹהֶיךָ עַל
הָאָרֶץ הַטֹּבָה אֲשֶׁר נָתַן לָךְ. בָּרוּךְ אַתָּה יהוה עַל הָאָרֶץ
וְעַל הַמָּזוֹן:

רַחֶם נָא יהוה אֱלֹהֵינוּ, עַל יִשְׂרָאֵל עַמֶּךָ, וְעַל יְרוּשָׁלַיִם
עִירֶךָ, וְעַל צִיּוֹן מִשְׁכַּן כְּבוֹדֶךָ, וְעַל מַלְכוּת בֵּית דָּוִד
מְשִׁיחֶךָ, וְעַל הַבַּיִת הַגָּדוֹל וְהַקָּדוֹשׁ שֶׁנִּקְרָא שִׁמְךָ עָלָיו.

BLESSED *are You, Hashem, our God, King of the universe, Who feeds the whole world in His benevolence, with graciousness, with kindness and with compassion. He "gives food to all flesh, for His kindness is forever" (Tehillim 136:25). And in His great benevolence, we have never lacked food, nor will we ever lack food, for the sake of His great Name, for He is God, Who feeds and sustains all, is benevolent to all, and prepares food for all His creatures that He created. Blessed are You, Hashem, Who provides food for all.*

WE *thank You, Hashem, our God, for having bestowed upon our ancestors a precious, good and spacious land; for having brought us out, Hashem our God, from the land of Egypt and redeeming us from the house of bondage; for Your covenant, which You have sealed in our flesh, and for Your Torah, which You have taught us; for Your statutes, which You have made known to us; for life, grace, and kindness which You have graciously granted us; and for our eating of the food that You provide and sustain us with constantly, every day, at all times, and at every hour.*

FOR *everything, Hashem our God, we are thankful to You and bless You. May Your Name always be blessed in the mouth of every living being, forever. Thus it is written: "And you will eat and become sated, and you shall bless Hashem your God for the fine land that He has given you" (Devarim 8:10). Blessed are You, Hashem, for the land and for the food.*

HAVE *mercy, Hashem our God, upon Israel Your People, upon Jerusalem Your city, upon Zion the abode of Your glory, upon the kingship of the House of David Your anointed one, and upon the great and holy Temple with which Your Name is associated. Our God, our Father! Provide for us, nourish us, sustain us,*

אֱלֹהֵינוּ אָבִינוּ, רְעֵנוּ זוּנֵנוּ פַּרְנְסֵנוּ וְכַלְכְּלֵנוּ וְהַרְוִיחֵנוּ,
וְהַרְוַח לָנוּ יהוה אֱלֹהֵינוּ מְהֵרָה מִכָּל צָרוֹתֵינוּ. וְנָא
אַל תַּצְרִיכֵנוּ יהוה אֱלֹהֵינוּ לֹא לִידֵי מַתְּנַת בָּשָׂר וָדָם,
וְלֹא לִידֵי הַלְוָאָתָם, כִּי אִם לְיָדְךָ הַמְּלֵאָה הַפְּתוּחָה
הַקְּדוֹשָׁה וְהָרְחָבָה, שֶׁלֹּא נֵבוֹשׁ וְלֹא נִכָּלֵם לְעוֹלָם
וָעֶד:

On Shabbos, the following paragraph is added:

רְצֵה וְהַחֲלִיצֵנוּ יהוה אֱלֹהֵינוּ בְּמִצְוֹתֶיךָ, וּבְמִצְוַת יוֹם הַשְּׁבִיעִי הַשַּׁבָּת
הַגָּדוֹל וְהַקָּדוֹשׁ הַזֶּה, כִּי יוֹם זֶה גָּדוֹל וְקָדוֹשׁ הוּא לְפָנֶיךָ, לִשְׁבָּת בּוֹ
וְלָנוּחַ בּוֹ בְּאַהֲבָה כְּמִצְוַת רְצוֹנֶךָ, וּבִרְצוֹנְךָ הָנִיחַ לָנוּ יהוה אֱלֹהֵינוּ שֶׁלֹּא
תְהֵא צָרָה וְיָגוֹן וַאֲנָחָה בְּיוֹם מְנוּחָתֵנוּ, וְהַרְאֵנוּ יהוה אֱלֹהֵינוּ בְּנֶחָמַת
צִיּוֹן עִירֶךָ וּבְבִנְיַן יְרוּשָׁלַיִם עִיר קָדְשֶׁךָ, כִּי אַתָּה הוּא בַּעַל הַיְשׁוּעוֹת
וּבַעַל הַנֶּחָמוֹת:

אֱלֹהֵינוּ וֵאלֹהֵי אֲבוֹתֵינוּ, יַעֲלֶה וְיָבֹא וְיַגִּיעַ וְיֵרָאֶה
וְיֵרָצֶה וְיִשָּׁמַע וְיִפָּקֵד וְיִזָּכֵר זִכְרוֹנֵנוּ וּפִקְדוֹנֵנוּ, וְזִכְרוֹן
אֲבוֹתֵינוּ, וְזִכְרוֹן מָשִׁיחַ בֶּן דָּוִד עַבְדֶּךָ, וְזִכְרוֹן יְרוּשָׁלַיִם
עִיר קָדְשֶׁךָ, וְזִכְרוֹן כָּל עַמְּךָ בֵּית יִשְׂרָאֵל לְפָנֶיךָ, לִפְלֵיטָה
לְטוֹבָה לְחֵן וּלְחֶסֶד וּלְרַחֲמִים לְחַיִּים וּלְשָׁלוֹם בְּיוֹם חַג
הַמַּצּוֹת הַזֶּה, זָכְרֵנוּ יהוה אֱלֹהֵינוּ בּוֹ לְטוֹבָה, וּפָקְדֵנוּ בוֹ
לִבְרָכָה, וְהוֹשִׁיעֵנוּ בוֹ לְחַיִּים, וּבִדְבַר יְשׁוּעָה וְרַחֲמִים
חוּס וְחָנֵּנוּ וְרַחֵם עָלֵינוּ וְהוֹשִׁיעֵנוּ, כִּי אֵלֶיךָ עֵינֵינוּ, כִּי
אֵל מֶלֶךְ חַנּוּן וְרַחוּם אָתָּה:

support us, and relieve us; and speedily grant us relief, Hashem our God, from all our troubles. And do not make us dependent, Hashem our God, upon gifts of mortal men nor upon their loans—but only upon Your full, open, holy, and bountiful hand, that we may never be ashamed or embarrassed.

On Shabbos, the following paragraph is added:

May it please You, Hashem our God, to grant us strength through Your commandments, and through the commandment of the seventh day—this great and holy Sabbath. For this day is a great and holy one before You, to refrain from work and to rest on it with love, in accordance with the commandment of Your will. And may it be Your will, Hashem, our God, to grant us tranquility, that there should be no misfortune, sorrow, or anguish on our day of our rest. And allow us to behold, Hashem our God, the solace of Zion Your city and the rebuilding of Jerusalem Your holy city, for You are the Master of salvations and the Master of consolations.

OUR *God and God of our fathers! May they ascend, come and reach, be seen and accepted, heard, recalled, and remembered before You—the remembrance and recollection of us, the remembrance of our fathers, the remembrance of the Messiah, the descendant of David Your servant, the remembrance of Jerusalem Your holy city, and the remembrance of all Your People the House of Israel, for deliverance, welfare, grace, kindness, mercy, life, and peace, on this day of the Festival of Matzos. Remember us on it, Hashem, our God, for good; recall us on it for a blessing; and spare us on it for life. And with a word of salvation and compassion, pity us and be gracious to us, and have mercy upon us and save us; for our eyes are [lifted] towards You, for You are a gracious and merciful God (and King).*

וּבְנֵה יְרוּשָׁלַיִם עִיר הַקֹּדֶשׁ בִּמְהֵרָה בְיָמֵינוּ.
בָּרוּךְ אַתָּה יהוה בּוֹנֵה בְרַחֲמָיו יְרוּשָׁלָיִם, אָמֵן:

בָּרוּךְ אַתָּה יהוה אֱלֹהֵינוּ מֶלֶךְ הָעוֹלָם, הָאֵל אָבִינוּ
מַלְכֵּנוּ אַדִּירֵנוּ בּוֹרְאֵנוּ גּוֹאֲלֵנוּ יוֹצְרֵנוּ קְדוֹשֵׁנוּ קְדוֹשׁ
יַעֲקֹב, רוֹעֵנוּ רוֹעֵה יִשְׂרָאֵל, הַמֶּלֶךְ הַטּוֹב וְהַמֵּטִיב לַכֹּל,
שֶׁבְּכָל יוֹם וָיוֹם הוּא הֵטִיב הוּא מֵטִיב הוּא יֵיטִיב לָנוּ,
הוּא גְמָלָנוּ הוּא גוֹמְלֵנוּ הוּא יִגְמְלֵנוּ לָעַד, לְחֵן וּלְחֶסֶד
וּלְרַחֲמִים וּלְרֶוַח הַצָּלָה וְהַצְלָחָה, בְּרָכָה וִישׁוּעָה נֶחָמָה
פַּרְנָסָה וְכַלְכָּלָה, וְרַחֲמִים וְחַיִּים וְשָׁלוֹם וְכָל טוֹב, וּמִכָּל
טוּב לְעוֹלָם אַל יְחַסְּרֵנוּ:

הָרַחֲמָן, הוּא יִמְלוֹךְ עָלֵינוּ לְעוֹלָם וָעֶד:

הָרַחֲמָן, הוּא יִתְבָּרַךְ בַּשָּׁמַיִם וּבָאָרֶץ:

הָרַחֲמָן, הוּא יִשְׁתַּבַּח לְדוֹר דּוֹרִים, וְיִתְפָּאַר בָּנוּ
לָעַד וּלְנֵצַח נְצָחִים, וְיִתְהַדַּר בָּנוּ לָעַד וּלְעוֹלְמֵי עוֹלָמִים:

הָרַחֲמָן, הוּא יְפַרְנְסֵנוּ בְּכָבוֹד:

הָרַחֲמָן, הוּא יִשְׁבּוֹר עֹל גָּלוּתֵנוּ מֵעַל צַוָּארֵנוּ וְהוּא
יוֹלִיכֵנוּ קוֹמְמִיּוּת לְאַרְצֵנוּ:

הָרַחֲמָן, הוּא יִשְׁלַח לָנוּ בְּרָכָה מְרֻבָּה בַּבַּיִת הַזֶּה,
וְעַל שֻׁלְחָן זֶה שֶׁאָכַלְנוּ עָלָיו:

הָרַחֲמָן, הוּא יִשְׁלַח לָנוּ אֶת אֵלִיָּהוּ הַנָּבִיא זָכוּר
לַטּוֹב וִיבַשֶּׂר לָנוּ בְּשׂוֹרוֹת טוֹבוֹת יְשׁוּעוֹת וְנֶחָמוֹת:

Rebuild Jerusalem the holy city speedily in our days. Blessed are You, Hashem, Who rebuilds Jerusalem in His mercy. Amen.

BLESSED *are You, Hashem, our God, King of the universe, the God, our Father, our Mighty One, our Creator, our Redeemer, our Maker, our Holy One, the Holy One of Yaakov, our Shepherd, the Shepherd of Israel, the King who is benevolent and bestows benevolence upon all, Who each and every day has done good for us, does good for us, and will do good for us; He has bestowed upon us, bestows upon us, and will forever bestow upon us grace, kindness and mercy, relief, salvation, success, blessing, deliverance, consolation, sustenance and nourishment, mercy, life, peace and all goodness; and may He never allow us any lack of bounty.*

MAY *the Merciful One reign over us forever and ever.*

MAY *the Merciful One be blessed in heaven and on earth.*

MAY *the Merciful One be praised for all generations, and may He be glorified among us forever and ever, and may He be honored among us for all eternity.*

MAY *the Merciful One grant us honorable sustenance.*

MAY *the Merciful One break off our yoke from our necks and lead us upright to our land.*

MAY *the Merciful One send us abundant blessing into this house, and upon this table at which we have eaten.*

MAY *the Merciful One send us Elijah the Prophet—may he be remembered for a blessing—to proclaim good tidings of salvation and consolation to us.*

הָרַחֲמָן, הוּא יְבָרֵךְ אֶת [אָבִי מוֹרִי] בַּעַל הַבַּיִת הַזֶּה
וְאֶת [אִמִּי מוֹרָתִי] בַּעֲלַת הַבַּיִת הַזֶּה, אוֹתָם וְאֶת בֵּיתָם
וְאֶת זַרְעָם וְאֶת כָּל אֲשֶׁר לָהֶם, אוֹתָנוּ וְאֶת כָּל אֲשֶׁר לָנוּ,
כְּמוֹ שֶׁנִּתְבָּרְכוּ אֲבוֹתֵינוּ אַבְרָהָם יִצְחָק וְיַעֲקֹב בַּכֹּל מִכֹּל
כֹּל, כֵּן יְבָרֵךְ אוֹתָנוּ כֻּלָּנוּ יַחַד, בִּבְרָכָה שְׁלֵמָה, וְנֹאמַר אָמֵן:
בַּמָּרוֹם יְלַמְּדוּ עֲלֵיהֶם וְעָלֵינוּ זְכוּת שֶׁתְּהֵא לְמִשְׁמֶרֶת
שָׁלוֹם, וְנִשָּׂא בְרָכָה מֵאֵת יהוה וּצְדָקָה מֵאֱלֹהֵי יִשְׁעֵנוּ,
וְנִמְצָא חֵן וְשֵׂכֶל טוֹב בְּעֵינֵי אֱלֹהִים וְאָדָם:

On Shabbos, the following is added:

הָרַחֲמָן, הוּא יַנְחִילֵנוּ יוֹם שֶׁכֻּלּוֹ שַׁבָּת וּמְנוּחָה לְחַיֵּי הָעוֹלָמִים:

הָרַחֲמָן הוּא יַנְחִילֵנוּ יוֹם שֶׁכֻּלּוֹ טוֹב. יוֹם שֶׁכֻּלּוֹ אָרוּךְ,
יוֹם שֶׁצַּדִּיקִים יוֹשְׁבִים וְעַטְרוֹתֵיהֶם בְּרָאשֵׁיהֶם וְנֶהֱנִים
מִזִּיו הַשְּׁכִינָה, וִיהִי חֶלְקֵנוּ עִמָּהֶם:
הָרַחֲמָן, הוּא יְזַכֵּנוּ לִימוֹת הַמָּשִׁיחַ וּלְחַיֵּי הָעוֹלָם הַבָּא:
מִגְדּוֹל יְשׁוּעוֹת מַלְכּוֹ וְעֹשֶׂה חֶסֶד לִמְשִׁיחוֹ לְדָוִד
וּלְזַרְעוֹ עַד עוֹלָם: עֹשֶׂה שָׁלוֹם בִּמְרוֹמָיו הוּא יַעֲשֶׂה
שָׁלוֹם עָלֵינוּ וְעַל כָּל יִשְׂרָאֵל, וְאִמְרוּ אָמֵן:
יְראוּ אֶת יהוה קְדֹשָׁיו, כִּי אֵין מַחְסוֹר לִירֵאָיו:
כְּפִירִים רָשׁוּ וְרָעֵבוּ, וְדֹרְשֵׁי יהוה לֹא יַחְסְרוּ כָל טוֹב:
הוֹדוּ לַיהוה כִּי טוֹב, כִּי לְעוֹלָם חַסְדּוֹ: פּוֹתֵחַ אֶת יָדֶךָ,

MAY the Merciful One bless [my father, my teacher,] the master of this house / and [my mother, my teacher,] the lady of this house—them, their household, their offspring, and all that is theirs, as well as us and all that is ours. Just as our forefathers Avraham, Yitzchak, and Yaakov, were blessed with everything, from everything, and everything, so may He bless all of us together, with a complete blessing. And let us say Amen.

ON High, may there be invoked merit for them and for us, which will serve them as a safeguard for peace. And may we receive blessing from the Hashem and kindness from the God of our salvation, and may we find grace and good repute in the eyes of God and man.

On Shabbos, the following is added:

May the Merciful One allow us to inherit that day that will be a complete Sabbath and rest, for eternal life.

MAY the Merciful One allow us to inherit that day that will be total goodness, that day when the righteous sit with their crowns of glory on their heads, benefiting from the splendor of the Divine Presence; and may our portion be among them.

MAY the Merciful One grant us the privilege of experiencing the Messianic era and the life of the Next World. He is a tower of His king's salvation, and does kindness for His anointed one, for David and his descendants forever.

HE Who makes peace in His heights—may He make peace over us and over all Israel. And say, Amen.

FEAR Hashem, you, His holy ones, for those who fear Him want for nothing. Young lions may be deprived and go hungry, but those who seek out Hashem shall not lack any goodness.

וּמַשְׂבִּיעַ לְכָל חַי רָצוֹן: בָּרוּךְ הַגֶּבֶר אֲשֶׁר יִבְטַח בַּיהוה,
וְהָיָה יְהוָה מִבְטַחוֹ: נַעַר הָיִיתִי גַּם זָקַנְתִּי, וְלֹא רָאִיתִי
צַדִּיק נֶעֱזָב וְזַרְעוֹ מְבַקֶּשׁ לָחֶם: יהוה עֹז לְעַמּוֹ יִתֵּן,
יהוה יְבָרֵךְ אֶת עַמּוֹ בַשָּׁלוֹם:

בָּרוּךְ אַתָּה יהוה אֱלֹהֵינוּ מֶלֶךְ הָעוֹלָם,
בּוֹרֵא פְּרִי הַגָּפֶן:

The third cup of wine is now drunk, while reclining on the left side.

The "Cup of Eliyahu" is now filled. There are those who pour the fourth cup of wine at this point as well. (Others pour it after the recitation of these verses.)

The door of the house is opened as the following verses are recited. (Some have the custom to rise while reciting these passages.)

שְׁפֹךְ חֲמָתְךָ אֶל הַגּוֹיִם אֲשֶׁר לֹא יְדָעוּךָ וְעַל מַמְלָכוֹת
אֲשֶׁר בְּשִׁמְךָ לֹא קָרָאוּ: כִּי אָכַל אֶת יַעֲקֹב וְאֶת נָוֵהוּ
הֵשַׁמּוּ: שְׁפָךְ עֲלֵיהֶם זַעְמֶךָ וַחֲרוֹן אַפְּךָ יַשִּׂיגֵם: תִּרְדֹּף
בְּאַף וְתַשְׁמִידֵם מִתַּחַת שְׁמֵי יהוה:

The door is closed.

Who might surprise you when you open the door for שְׁפֹךְ חֲמָתְךָ (besides for Eliyahu HaNavi)?

In some places, the custom was that one of the participants at the Seder would hide outside and then enter the house when the door was opened for שְׁפֹךְ חֲמָתְךָ. The reason for this *minhag* was to demonstrate our firm belief in the coming of Mashiach (*Yosef Ometz* 788).

Some speculate that the origins for the custom of opening the door can be traced to a period in history when the Jews were subject to persecutions. When they would reach שְׁפֹךְ חֲמָתְךָ in their recital of

Give thanks to Hashem, for He is good, for His kindness is for-
ever. You open Your hand and satisfy the desire of every living
thing. Blessed be the man who trusts in Hashem and makes
Hashem his security. I was once a boy, and have also grown old,
and I have never seen a righteous man forsaken or his offspring
begging for bread. Hashem will give strength to His People;
Hashem will bless His People with peace.

Blessed are You, Hashem, our God, King of the universe, who creates the fruit of the vine.

The third cup of wine is now drunk, while reclining on the left side.

The "Cup of Eliyahu" is now filled. There are those who pour the fourth cup of wine at this point as well. (Others pour it after the recitation of these verses.)

The door of the house is opened as the following verses are recited. (Some have the custom to rise while reciting these passages.)

POUR *out Your wrath upon the nations that did not acknowl-*
edge You and upon the kingdoms that did not call upon Your
Name. For they have devoured Yaakov and laid waste his abode
(Tehillim 79:6–7). Pour out Your fury upon them, and let the
heat of Your anger overtake them (ibid. 69:25). Pursue [them]
with anger, and destroy them from beneath the heavens of
Hashem (Eichah 3:66).

The door is closed.

the Haggadah, they would open the door to check that there were
no informers standing outside their home. If an informer would tell
the ruling authorities that the Jews were asking Hashem to punish
their enemies, it would have led to further oppression of the Jews.
Therefore, they checked to make sure no one was listening while they
said שְׁפוֹךְ חֲמָתְךָ (*Haggadah Sheleimah*, p. 180).

הלל

The fourth cup of wine is poured. The remaining part of Hallel is now recited:

לֹא לָנוּ יהוה לֹא לָנוּ, כִּי לְשִׁמְךָ תֵּן כָּבוֹד עַל חַסְדְּךָ עַל אֲמִתֶּךָ: לָמָּה יֹאמְרוּ הַגּוֹיִם, אַיֵּה נָא אֱלֹהֵיהֶם: וֵאלֹהֵינוּ בַשָּׁמַיִם, כֹּל אֲשֶׁר חָפֵץ עָשָׂה: עֲצַבֵּיהֶם כֶּסֶף וְזָהָב, מַעֲשֵׂה יְדֵי אָדָם: פֶּה לָהֶם וְלֹא יְדַבֵּרוּ, עֵינַיִם לָהֶם וְלֹא יִרְאוּ: אָזְנַיִם לָהֶם וְלֹא יִשְׁמָעוּ, אַף לָהֶם וְלֹא יְרִיחוּן: יְדֵיהֶם וְלֹא יְמִישׁוּן רַגְלֵיהֶם וְלֹא יְהַלֵּכוּ, לֹא יֶהְגּוּ בִּגְרוֹנָם: כְּמוֹהֶם יִהְיוּ עֹשֵׂיהֶם, כֹּל אֲשֶׁר בֹּטֵחַ בָּהֶם: יִשְׂרָאֵל בְּטַח בַּיהוה, עֶזְרָם וּמָגִנָּם הוּא: בֵּית אַהֲרֹן בִּטְחוּ בַיהוה, עֶזְרָם וּמָגִנָּם הוּא: יִרְאֵי יהוה בִּטְחוּ בַיהוה, עֶזְרָם וּמָגִנָּם הוּא:

יהוה זְכָרָנוּ יְבָרֵךְ, יְבָרֵךְ אֶת בֵּית יִשְׂרָאֵל, יְבָרֵךְ אֶת בֵּית אַהֲרֹן: יְבָרֵךְ יִרְאֵי יהוה, הַקְּטַנִּים עִם הַגְּדֹלִים: יֹסֵף

Which two *berachos* do some authorities require one to say on *Hallel*?

Some authorities say that before the first part of *Hallel*, we recite the *berachah* of לִקְרֹא אֶת הַהַלֵּל, and before the second part of *Hallel* (after *Birkas Hamazon*) we say לִגְמֹר אֶת הַהַלֵּל, *to finish reciting the Hallel* (*Shibolei HaLeket* 218, *Me'iri*, *Pesachim* 117b. According to the *Smag, Asin 41*, one would recite לִקְרֹא אֶת הַהַלֵּל twice). These opinions are not accepted in the final halachah, and we therefore do not make a *berachah* on *Hallel* (*Chok Yaakov* 480:1). One of the reasons we do not make a *berachah* on *Hallel* is because *Hallel* is split in two, and we do not make a *berachah* twice on a mitzvah (*Ra'aviyah* 525). Also, לְפִיכָךְ

HALLEL

The fourth cup of wine is poured. The remaining part of Hallel is now recited:

(Psalm 115)

NOT *for us, Hashem, not for us, but for Your Name give glory, for the sake of Your kindness and Your truth. Why should the nations say, "Where, now, is their God?" But our God is in heaven; He does whatever He desires. Their idols are silver and gold, the product of human hands. They have a mouth but cannot speak; they have eyes but cannot see; they have ears but cannot hear; they have a nose but cannot smell; they have hands but cannot feel; they have feet but cannot walk; they can utter no sound with their throat. May those who make them be like them—all those who trust in them! Israel, trust in Hashem; He is their help and their shield. House of Aaron, trust in Hashem; He is their help and their shield. You who fear Hashem, trust in Hashem; He is their help and their shield.*

HASHEM, *Who has always remembered us, will bless—He will bless the House of Israel, He will bless the House of Aaron, He will bless those who fear Hashem, the smaller ones along with the*

אֲנַחְנוּ חַיָּבִים לְהוֹדוֹת, the praises we say before reciting the first part of *Hallel*, can be considered the *berachah* over *Hallel* (*Orchos Chayim* quoted in *Otzros HaHaggadah*, p. 605).

If you stand up, you might drop the cup! What does this refer to?

Normally, one is meant to recite *Hallel* while standing (*Shulchan Aruch* 422:7). On Seder night, however, we say it while sitting down. One of the reasons for this is because if one stands up to say *Hallel*, he might drop the cup of wine in his hands (*Shibolei HaLeket* 173).

יְהֹוָה עֲלֵיכֶם, עֲלֵיכֶם וְעַל בְּנֵיכֶם: בְּרוּכִים אַתֶּם לַיהֹוָה,
עֹשֵׂה שָׁמַיִם וָאָרֶץ: הַשָּׁמַיִם שָׁמַיִם לַיהֹוָה, וְהָאָרֶץ נָתַן
לִבְנֵי אָדָם: לֹא הַמֵּתִים יְהַלְלוּ יָהּ, וְלֹא כָּל יֹרְדֵי דוּמָה:
וַאֲנַחְנוּ נְבָרֵךְ יָהּ, מֵעַתָּה וְעַד עוֹלָם, הַלְלוּיָהּ:

אָהַבְתִּי כִּי יִשְׁמַע יְהֹוָה, אֶת קוֹלִי תַּחֲנוּנָי: כִּי הִטָּה
אָזְנוֹ לִי, וּבְיָמַי אֶקְרָא: אֲפָפוּנִי חֶבְלֵי מָוֶת, וּמְצָרֵי
שְׁאוֹל מְצָאוּנִי, צָרָה וְיָגוֹן אֶמְצָא: וּבְשֵׁם יְהֹוָה אֶקְרָא,
אָנָּה יְהֹוָה מַלְּטָה נַפְשִׁי: חַנּוּן יְהֹוָה וְצַדִּיק, וֵאלֹהֵינוּ
מְרַחֵם: שֹׁמֵר פְּתָאיִם יְהֹוָה, דַּלּוֹתִי וְלִי יְהוֹשִׁיעַ: שׁוּבִי
נַפְשִׁי לִמְנוּחָיְכִי, כִּי יְהֹוָה גָּמַל עָלָיְכִי: כִּי חִלַּצְתָּ נַפְשִׁי
מִמָּוֶת, אֶת עֵינִי מִן דִּמְעָה אֶת רַגְלִי מִדֶּחִי: אֶתְהַלֵּךְ
לִפְנֵי יְהֹוָה, בְּאַרְצוֹת הַחַיִּים: הֶאֱמַנְתִּי כִּי אֲדַבֵּר, אֲנִי
עָנִיתִי מְאֹד: אֲנִי אָמַרְתִּי בְחָפְזִי, כָּל הָאָדָם כֹּזֵב:

מָה אָשִׁיב לַיהֹוָה, כָּל תַּגְמוּלוֹהִי עָלָי: כּוֹס יְשׁוּעוֹת
אֶשָּׂא, וּבְשֵׁם יְהֹוָה אֶקְרָא: נְדָרַי לַיהֹוָה אֲשַׁלֵּם, נֶגְדָה
נָּא לְכָל עַמּוֹ: יָקָר בְּעֵינֵי יְהֹוָה, הַמָּוְתָה לַחֲסִידָיו:
אָנָּה יְהֹוָה כִּי אֲנִי עַבְדֶּךָ, אֲנִי עַבְדְּךָ בֶּן אֲמָתֶךָ, פִּתַּחְתָּ
לְמוֹסֵרָי: לְךָ אֶזְבַּח זֶבַח תּוֹדָה וּבְשֵׁם יְהֹוָה אֶקְרָא: נְדָרַי
לַיהֹוָה אֲשַׁלֵּם, נֶגְדָה נָּא לְכָל עַמּוֹ: בְּחַצְרוֹת בֵּית יְהֹוָה,
בְּתוֹכֵכִי יְרוּשָׁלַיִם, הַלְלוּיָהּ:

הַלְלוּ אֶת יְהֹוָה כָּל גּוֹיִם, שַׁבְּחוּהוּ כָּל הָאֻמִּים: כִּי
גָבַר עָלֵינוּ חַסְדּוֹ, וֶאֱמֶת יְהֹוָה לְעוֹלָם, הַלְלוּיָהּ:

greater ones. Hashem will increase you—you and your children. Blessed are you for Hashem, the Maker of heaven and earth. The heavens are the heavens of Hashem, but the earth He gave to mankind. The dead do not praise God, nor do those who go down to the grave. But we will bless God, from now to eternity. Halleluyah!

(Psalm 116)

I *loved that Hashem hears my voice, my prayers. For He inclined His ear to me, so all my days I will call [Him]. The pains of death encompassed me, and the anguish of dying came upon me, I encounter misfortune and sorrow—and I call out in the Name of Hashem, "Please, Hashem, rescue my life!" Hashem is gracious and righteous; and our God shows compassion. Hashem watches over simple people; when I sink low He will save me. Return, my soul, to your rest, for Hashem has dealt kindly with you. For You have released my soul from death, my eyes from tears, my foot from stumbling. I will walk before Hashem in the lands of the living. I had faith when I said, "I am greatly distressed," I said in my haste, "All men are deceitful."*

WITH *what can I repay Hashem for all His kindness to me? I will raise a cup of salvation and call the Name of Hashem. I will fulfill my vows to Hashem now, in the presence of all His People. The death of His pious ones is difficult in the eyes of Hashem. I thank You, Hashem, for I am Your servant; I am Your servant, the son of Your maidservant, and You have broken open my bonds. I will sacrifice a thanksgiving offering to You, and I will call the Name of Hashem. I will fulfill my vows to Hashem now, in the presence of all His People, in the courtyards of the Temple of Hashem, in the midst of Jerusalem. Halleluyah!*

(Psalm 117)

PRAISE *Hashem, all nations! Laud Him, all peoples! For His kindness has overwhelmed us, and the truth of Hashem is forever. Halleluyah!*

If there are three adult males present at the Seder, the following four verses are recited
responsively:

הוֹדוּ לַיהוה כִּי טוֹב   כִּי לְעוֹלָם חַסְדּוֹ:

יֹאמַר נָא יִשְׂרָאֵל   כִּי לְעוֹלָם חַסְדּוֹ:

יֹאמְרוּ נָא בֵית אַהֲרֹן   כִּי לְעוֹלָם חַסְדּוֹ:

יֹאמְרוּ נָא יִרְאֵי יהוה   כִּי לְעוֹלָם חַסְדּוֹ:

מִן הַמֵּצַר קָרָאתִי יָּהּ, עָנָנִי בַמֶּרְחָב יָהּ: יהוה לִי
לֹא אִירָא, מַה יַּעֲשֶׂה לִי אָדָם: יהוה לִי בְּעֹזְרָי, וַאֲנִי
אֶרְאֶה בְשֹׂנְאָי: טוֹב לַחֲסוֹת בַּיהוה, מִבְּטֹחַ בָּאָדָם:
טוֹב לַחֲסוֹת בַּיהוה, מִבְּטֹחַ בִּנְדִיבִים: כָּל גּוֹיִם סְבָבוּנִי,
בְּשֵׁם יהוה כִּי אֲמִילַם: סַבּוּנִי גַם סְבָבוּנִי, בְּשֵׁם יהוה
כִּי אֲמִילַם: סַבּוּנִי כִדְבוֹרִים דֹּעֲכוּ כְּאֵשׁ קוֹצִים, בְּשֵׁם
יהוה כִּי אֲמִילַם: דָּחֹה דְחִיתַנִי לִנְפֹּל, וַיהוה עֲזָרָנִי: עָזִּי
וְזִמְרָת יָהּ, וַיְהִי לִי לִישׁוּעָה: קוֹל רִנָּה וִישׁוּעָה בְּאָהֳלֵי
צַדִּיקִים, יְמִין יהוה עֹשָׂה חָיִל: יְמִין יהוה רוֹמֵמָה, יְמִין
יהוה עֹשָׂה חָיִל: לֹא אָמוּת כִּי אֶחְיֶה, וַאֲסַפֵּר מַעֲשֵׂי
יָהּ: יַסֹּר יִסְּרַנִּי יָּהּ, וְלַמָּוֶת לֹא נְתָנָנִי: פִּתְחוּ לִי שַׁעֲרֵי
צֶדֶק, אָבֹא בָם אוֹדֶה יָהּ: זֶה הַשַּׁעַר לַיהוה, צַדִּיקִים
יָבֹאוּ בוֹ: אוֹדְךָ כִּי עֲנִיתָנִי, וַתְּהִי לִי לִישׁוּעָה: אוֹדְךָ כִּי
עֲנִיתָנִי, וַתְּהִי לִי לִישׁוּעָה: אֶבֶן מָאֲסוּ הַבּוֹנִים, הָיְתָה
לְרֹאשׁ פִּנָּה: אֶבֶן מָאֲסוּ הַבּוֹנִים, הָיְתָה לְרֹאשׁ פִּנָּה:
מֵאֵת יהוה הָיְתָה זֹּאת, הִיא נִפְלָאת בְּעֵינֵינוּ: מֵאֵת

If there are three adult males present at the Seder, the following four verses are recited responsively:

(Psalm 118)

GIVE *thanks to Hashem: For He is good, for His kindness is forever.*

LET *Israel say:*   *For His kindness is forever.*

LET *the House of Aaron say:*   *For His kindness is forever.*

LET *those who fear Hashem say:*   *For His kindness is forever.*

OUT *of the narrow straits I called to God; God answered me by [granting me] spaciousness. Hashem is with me, I shall not fear; what can man do to me? Hashem is with me among those who help me, and I will see my enemies' [downfall]. It is better to seek shelter with Hashem than to trust in man; it is better to seek shelter in Hashem than to trust in nobles. If all the nations surround me, I will cut them down in the Name of Hashem. If they surround me and they encompass me, I will cut them down in the Name of Hashem. If they surround me like bees, they are extinguished like a fire of thorns; I will cut them down in the Name of Hashem. You may push me repeatedly to make me fall, but Hashem helps me. God is my strength and my song, and He has always been my salvation. The sound of shouts of joy and salvation is in the tents of the righteous: "The right hand of Hashem acts valiantly. The right hand of Hashem is exalted; the right hand of Hashem acts valiantly!" I shall not die, but I shall live, and I shall relate the deeds of God. God may chastise me, but He has not given me over to death. Open for me the gates of righteousness; I will enter them and give thanks to God. This is the gate of Hashem; the righteous will enter it. I give thanks to You for You have answered me, and You have been my salvation. I give*

יהוה הָיְתָה זֹּאת, הִיא נִפְלָאת בְּעֵינֵינוּ: זֶה הַיּוֹם עָשָׂה
יהוה, נָגִילָה וְנִשְׂמְחָה בוֹ: זֶה הַיּוֹם עָשָׂה יהוה, נָגִילָה
וְנִשְׂמְחָה בוֹ:

If there are three adult males present at the Seder, the following four phrases are recited
responsively:

אָנָּא יהוה הוֹשִׁיעָה נָּא:

אָנָּא יהוה הוֹשִׁיעָה נָּא:

אָנָּא יהוה הַצְלִיחָה נָּא:

אָנָּא יהוה הַצְלִיחָה נָּא:

בָּרוּךְ הַבָּא בְּשֵׁם יהוה, בֵּרַכְנוּכֶם מִבֵּית יהוה: בָּרוּךְ
הַבָּא בְּשֵׁם יהוה, בֵּרַכְנוּכֶם מִבֵּית יהוה: אֵל יהוה וַיָּאֶר
לָנוּ, אִסְרוּ חַג בַּעֲבֹתִים עַד קַרְנוֹת הַמִּזְבֵּחַ: אֵל יהוה
וַיָּאֶר לָנוּ, אִסְרוּ חַג בַּעֲבֹתִים עַד קַרְנוֹת הַמִּזְבֵּחַ: אֵלִי
אַתָּה וְאוֹדֶךָּ, אֱלֹהַי אֲרוֹמְמֶךָּ: אֵלִי אַתָּה וְאוֹדֶךָּ, אֱלֹהַי
אֲרוֹמְמֶךָּ: הוֹדוּ לַיהוה כִּי טוֹב, כִּי לְעוֹלָם חַסְדּוֹ: הוֹדוּ
לַיהוה כִּי טוֹב, כִּי לְעוֹלָם חַסְדּוֹ:

יְהַלְלוּךָ יהוה אֱלֹהֵינוּ כָּל מַעֲשֶׂיךָ, וַחֲסִידֶיךָ צַדִּיקִים
עוֹשֵׂי רְצוֹנֶךָ, וְכָל עַמְּךָ בֵּית יִשְׂרָאֵל, בְּרִנָּה יוֹדוּ וִיבָרְכוּ
וִישַׁבְּחוּ וִיפָאֲרוּ וִירוֹמְמוּ וְיַעֲרִיצוּ וְיַקְדִּישׁוּ וְיַמְלִיכוּ
אֶת שִׁמְךָ מַלְכֵּנוּ, כִּי לְךָ טוֹב לְהוֹדוֹת וּלְשִׁמְךָ נָאֶה
לְזַמֵּר, כִּי מֵעוֹלָם וְעַד עוֹלָם אַתָּה אֵל:

thanks to You for You have answered me, and You have been my salvation. The stone rejected by the builders has become the main cornerstone. The stone rejected by the builders has become the main cornerstone. This took place because of Hashem; it is wondrous in our eyes. This took place because of Hashem; it is wondrous in our eyes. This is the day that Hashem has made, let us be glad and rejoice on it. This is the day that Hashem has made, let us be glad and rejoice on it.

If there are three adult males present at the Seder, the following four phrases are recited responsively:

PLEASE, *Hashem, save us now! Please, Hashem, save us now! Please, Hashem, grant us success now! Please, Hashem, grant us success now!*

BLESSED *is he who comes in the Name of Hashem; we bless you from the House of Hashem. Blessed is he who comes in the Name of Hashem; we bless you from the House of Hashem. Hashem is God, and He made light shine for us; bind the festival offering up to the corners of the altar. Hashem is God, and He made light shine for us; bind the festival offering up to the corners of the altar. You are my God and I will give thanks to You; my God, I will exalt You. You are my God and I will give thanks to You; my God, I will exalt You. Give thanks to Hashem, for He is good, for His kindness is forever. Give thanks to Hashem, for He is good, for His kindness is forever.*

ALL *Your works shall praise You, Hashem, our God, along with Your pious ones, the righteous who do Your will. And all Your People, the House of Israel, with shouts of joy, will give thanks, bless, laud, glorify, exalt, acclaim, sanctify, and proclaim the sovereignty of Your Name, our King. For it is good to give thanks to You, and it is befitting to sing to Your Name, for You are God for all eternity.*

כִּי לְעוֹלָם חַסְדּוֹ:	הוֹדוּ לַיהוה כִּי טוֹב
כִּי לְעוֹלָם חַסְדּוֹ:	הוֹדוּ לֵאלֹהֵי הָאֱלֹהִים
כִּי לְעוֹלָם חַסְדּוֹ:	הוֹדוּ לַאֲדֹנֵי הָאֲדֹנִים
כִּי לְעוֹלָם חַסְדּוֹ:	לְעֹשֵׂה נִפְלָאוֹת גְּדֹלוֹת לְבַדּוֹ
כִּי לְעוֹלָם חַסְדּוֹ:	לְעֹשֵׂה הַשָּׁמַיִם בִּתְבוּנָה
כִּי לְעוֹלָם חַסְדּוֹ:	לְרֹקַע הָאָרֶץ עַל הַמָּיִם
כִּי לְעוֹלָם חַסְדּוֹ:	לְעֹשֵׂה אוֹרִים גְּדֹלִים
כִּי לְעוֹלָם חַסְדּוֹ:	אֶת הַשֶּׁמֶשׁ לְמֶמְשֶׁלֶת בַּיּוֹם
כִּי לְעוֹלָם חַסְדּוֹ:	אֶת הַיָּרֵחַ וְכוֹכָבִים לְמֶמְשְׁלוֹת בַּלָּיְלָה
כִּי לְעוֹלָם חַסְדּוֹ:	לְמַכֵּה מִצְרַיִם בִּבְכוֹרֵיהֶם
כִּי לְעוֹלָם חַסְדּוֹ:	וַיּוֹצֵא יִשְׂרָאֵל מִתּוֹכָם
כִּי לְעוֹלָם חַסְדּוֹ:	בְּיָד חֲזָקָה וּבִזְרוֹעַ נְטוּיָה
כִּי לְעוֹלָם חַסְדּוֹ:	לְגֹזֵר יַם סוּף לִגְזָרִים
כִּי לְעוֹלָם חַסְדּוֹ:	וְהֶעֱבִיר יִשְׂרָאֵל בְּתוֹכוֹ
כִּי לְעוֹלָם חַסְדּוֹ:	וְנִעֵר פַּרְעֹה וְחֵילוֹ בְיַם סוּף
כִּי לְעוֹלָם חַסְדּוֹ:	לְמוֹלִיךְ עַמּוֹ בַּמִּדְבָּר
כִּי לְעוֹלָם חַסְדּוֹ:	לְמַכֵּה מְלָכִים גְּדֹלִים
כִּי לְעוֹלָם חַסְדּוֹ:	וַיַּהֲרֹג מְלָכִים אַדִּירִים

(Psalm 136—the "Great Hallel"):

Give thanks to Hashem, for He is good,
                    for His kindness is forever.

Give thanks to the God of gods,   *for His kindness is forever.*

Give thanks to the Lord of lords,   *for His kindness is forever.*

To the One Who alone does great wonders,
                    for His kindness is forever.

To the One Who made the heavens with understanding,
                    for His kindness is forever.

To the One Who stretched out the earth over the waters,
                    for His kindness is forever.

To the One Who made the great lights,   *for His kindness is forever.*

The sun to rule by day,   *for His kindness is forever.*

The moon and stars to rule by night,   *for His kindness is forever.*

To the One Who struck Egypt through their firstborn,
                    for His kindness is forever.

And took Israel out of their midst,   *for His kindness is forever.*

With a strong hand and with an outstretched arm,
                    for His kindness is forever.

To the One Who carved the Red Sea into sections,
                    for His kindness is forever.

And had Israel pass through it,   *for His kindness is forever.*

And stirred up Pharaoh and his army in the Red Sea,
                    for His kindness is forever.

To the One Who led His people through the desert,
                    for His kindness is forever.

To the One Who struck great kings, *for His kindness is forever.*

כִּי לְעוֹלָם חַסְדּוֹ:	לְסִיחוֹן מֶלֶךְ הָאֱמֹרִי
כִּי לְעוֹלָם חַסְדּוֹ:	וּלְעוֹג מֶלֶךְ הַבָּשָׁן
כִּי לְעוֹלָם חַסְדּוֹ:	וְנָתַן אַרְצָם לְנַחֲלָה
כִּי לְעוֹלָם חַסְדּוֹ:	נַחֲלָה לְיִשְׂרָאֵל עַבְדּוֹ
כִּי לְעוֹלָם חַסְדּוֹ:	שֶׁבְּשִׁפְלֵנוּ זָכַר לָנוּ
כִּי לְעוֹלָם חַסְדּוֹ:	וַיִּפְרְקֵנוּ מִצָּרֵינוּ
כִּי לְעוֹלָם חַסְדּוֹ:	נֹתֵן לֶחֶם לְכָל בָּשָׂר
כִּי לְעוֹלָם חַסְדּוֹ:	הוֹדוּ לְאֵל הַשָּׁמָיִם

נִשְׁמַת כָּל חַי תְּבָרֵךְ אֶת שִׁמְךָ יהוה אֱלֹהֵינוּ,
וְרוּחַ כָּל בָּשָׂר תְּפָאֵר וּתְרוֹמֵם זִכְרְךָ מַלְכֵּנוּ תָּמִיד,
מִן הָעוֹלָם וְעַד הָעוֹלָם אַתָּה אֵל, וּמִבַּלְעָדֶיךָ אֵין לָנוּ
מֶלֶךְ גּוֹאֵל וּמוֹשִׁיעַ, פּוֹדֶה וּמַצִּיל וּמְפַרְנֵס וּמְרַחֵם
בְּכָל עֵת צָרָה וְצוּקָה, אֵין לָנוּ מֶלֶךְ אֶלָּא אָתָּה. אֱלֹהֵי
הָרִאשׁוֹנִים וְהָאַחֲרוֹנִים, אֱלוֹהַּ כָּל בְּרִיּוֹת, אֲדוֹן כָּל
תּוֹלָדוֹת, הַמְהֻלָּל בְּרֹב הַתִּשְׁבָּחוֹת, הַמְנַהֵג עוֹלָמוֹ
בְּחֶסֶד וּבְרִיּוֹתָיו בְּרַחֲמִים. וַיהוה לֹא יָנוּם וְלֹא יִישָׁן,
הַמְּעוֹרֵר יְשֵׁנִים, וְהַמֵּקִיץ נִרְדָּמִים, וְהַמֵּשִׂיחַ אִלְּמִים,
וְהַמַּתִּיר אֲסוּרִים, וְהַסּוֹמֵךְ נוֹפְלִים, וְהַזּוֹקֵף כְּפוּפִים,
לְךָ לְבַדְּךָ אֲנַחְנוּ מוֹדִים. אִלּוּ פִינוּ מָלֵא שִׁירָה כַּיָּם,
וּלְשׁוֹנֵנוּ רִנָּה כַּהֲמוֹן גַּלָּיו, וְשִׂפְתוֹתֵינוּ שֶׁבַח כְּמֶרְחֲבֵי

And killed mighty kings,	for His kindness is forever.
Sichon, king of the Amorites,	for His kindness is forever.
And Og, king of Bashan,	for His kindness is forever.
And gave their land as an inheritance,	for His kindness is forever.
An inheritance to His servant Israel,	for His kindness is forever.

[To the One] Who remembered us when we were lowly,
for His kindness is forever.

And delivered us from our enemies,	for His kindness is forever.
He gives food to all flesh,	for His kindness is forever.
Give thanks to the God of heaven,	for His kindness is forever.

THE soul of every living being shall bless Your Name, Hashem, our God; and the spirit of all flesh shall always glorify and exalt Your remembrance, our King. For all eternity You are God, and other than You we have no king who redeems and saves us. You deliver, rescue, sustain, and show mercy in all times of trouble and distress; we have no king but You—the God of the first and of the last, God of all creatures, Lord of all generations, Who is lauded with a multitude of praises, Who guides His world with kindness and His creatures with compassion. Hashem neither slumbers nor sleeps; He awakens sleepers and rouses those who slumber; He makes the mute speak, releases the bound, supports those who are falling and straightens those who are bent over. To You alone do we give thanks.

EVEN if our mouths were as full with song as the sea, and our tongues [as full] with shouts of joy as the multitudes of its waves, and our lips [as full] with praise as the expanse of the sky, and our eyes as gleaming as the sun and the moon, and our hands as spread out as the eagles of heaven, and our feet

רָקִיעַ, וְעֵינֵינוּ מְאִירוֹת כַּשֶּׁמֶשׁ וְכַיָּרֵחַ, וְיָדֵינוּ פְרוּשׂוֹת כְּנִשְׁרֵי שָׁמָיִם, וְרַגְלֵינוּ קַלּוֹת כָּאַיָּלוֹת, אֵין אֲנַחְנוּ מַסְפִּיקִים לְהוֹדוֹת לְךָ יהוה אֱלֹהֵינוּ וֵאלֹהֵי אֲבוֹתֵינוּ, וּלְבָרֵךְ אֶת שְׁמֶךָ עַל אַחַת מֵאֶלֶף אֶלֶף אַלְפֵי אֲלָפִים וְרִבֵּי רְבָבוֹת פְּעָמִים, הַטּוֹבוֹת שֶׁעָשִׂיתָ עִם אֲבוֹתֵינוּ וְעִמָּנוּ. מִמִּצְרַיִם גְּאַלְתָּנוּ יהוה אֱלֹהֵינוּ וּמִבֵּית עֲבָדִים פְּדִיתָנוּ, בְּרָעָב זַנְתָּנוּ וּבְשָׂבָע כִּלְכַּלְתָּנוּ, מֵחֶרֶב הִצַּלְתָּנוּ וּמִדֶּבֶר מִלַּטְתָּנוּ, וּמֵחֳלָיִם רָעִים וְנֶאֱמָנִים דִּלִּיתָנוּ. עַד הֵנָּה עֲזָרוּנוּ רַחֲמֶיךָ וְלֹא עֲזָבוּנוּ חֲסָדֶיךָ, וְאַל תִּטְּשֵׁנוּ יהוה אֱלֹהֵינוּ לָנֶצַח. עַל כֵּן אֵבָרִים שֶׁפִּלַּגְתָּ בָּנוּ, וְרוּחַ וּנְשָׁמָה שֶׁנָּפַחְתָּ בְּאַפֵּינוּ, וְלָשׁוֹן אֲשֶׁר שַׂמְתָּ בְּפִינוּ, הֵן הֵם יוֹדוּ וִיבָרְכוּ וִישַׁבְּחוּ וִיפָאֲרוּ וִירוֹמְמוּ וְיַעֲרִיצוּ וְיַקְדִּישׁוּ וְיַמְלִיכוּ אֶת שִׁמְךָ מַלְכֵּנוּ. כִּי כָל פֶּה לְךָ יוֹדֶה, וְכָל לָשׁוֹן לְךָ תִשָּׁבַע, וְכָל בֶּרֶךְ לְךָ תִכְרַע, וְכָל קוֹמָה לְפָנֶיךָ תִשְׁתַּחֲוֶה, וְכָל לְבָבוֹת יִירָאוּךָ, וְכָל קֶרֶב וּכְלָיוֹת יְזַמְּרוּ לִשְׁמֶךָ, כַּדָּבָר שֶׁכָּתוּב, כָּל עַצְמוֹתַי תֹּאמַרְנָה יהוה מִי כָמוֹךָ. מַצִּיל עָנִי מֵחָזָק מִמֶּנּוּ, וְעָנִי וְאֶבְיוֹן מִגֹּזְלוֹ. מִי יִדְמֶה לָּךְ וּמִי יִשְׁוֶה לָּךְ וּמִי יַעֲרָךְ לָךְ, הָאֵל הַגָּדוֹל הַגִּבּוֹר וְהַנּוֹרָא אֵל עֶלְיוֹן, קוֹנֵה שָׁמַיִם וָאָרֶץ. נְהַלֶּלְךָ וּנְשַׁבֵּחֲךָ וּנְפָאֶרְךָ וּנְבָרֵךְ אֶת שֵׁם קָדְשֶׁךָ, כָּאָמוּר, לְדָוִד, בָּרְכִי נַפְשִׁי אֶת יהוה, וְכָל קְרָבַי אֶת שֵׁם קָדְשׁוֹ.

as swift as hinds—we would still be insufficient to thank You, Hashem, our God and God of our fathers, and to bless Your name for even one of the millions and billions of benevolent acts that You have done for our fathers and for us. You redeemed us from Egypt, Hashem, our God, and You delivered us from the house of bondage. You have fed us during famine and nourished us in times of plenty; You have saved us from the sword and rescued us from pestilence, and extricated us from dire and serious diseases. Up to now Your compassion has always helped us, and Your kindnesses have not left us; so too, do not abandon us, Hashem our God, forever more!

THEREFORE, *the limbs that You have supplied us with, and the spirit and soul that You have breathed into our nostrils, and the tongue that You have placed in our mouth—they shall all thank, bless, praise, glorify, exalt, acclaim, sanctify and proclaim the sovereignty of Your name, our King. For every mouth shall give thanks to You, every tongue shall swear allegiance to You, every knee shall kneel to You, every spine shall bow down before You, every heart shall fear You, and every organ and mind shall sing praises to Your Name, as it is written, "All my bones say: Hashem, who is like You? You save the poor man from those stronger than he, and the poor and needy man from one who tries to rob him" (Tehillim 35:10).*

WHO *can be likened to You, who is equal to You, who can be compared to You, the great, mighty, awesome God, supreme God, Possessor of heaven and earth! We shall praise You, laud You, and glorify You, and we will bless Your holy Name, as it says: "By David. Bless Hashem, O my soul, and all that is within me [bless] His holy Name" (Tehillim 103:1). You are the*

הָאֵל בְּתַעֲצֻמוֹת עֻזֶּךָ, הַגָּדוֹל בִּכְבוֹד שְׁמֶךָ, הַגִּבּוֹר לָנֶצַח וְהַנּוֹרָא בְּנוֹרְאוֹתֶיךָ,

הַמֶּלֶךְ הַיּוֹשֵׁב עַל כִּסֵּא רָם וְנִשָּׂא.

שׁוֹכֵן עַד מָרוֹם וְקָדוֹשׁ שְׁמוֹ, וְכָתוּב, רַנְּנוּ צַדִּיקִים בַּיהוה, לַיְשָׁרִים נָאוָה תְהִלָּה.

בְּפִי יְשָׁרִים תִּתְהַלָּל, וּבְדִבְרֵי צַדִּיקִים תִּתְבָּרַךְ, וּבִלְשׁוֹן חֲסִידִים תִּתְרוֹמָם, וּבְקֶרֶב קְדוֹשִׁים תִּתְקַדָּשׁ.

וּבְמַקְהֲלוֹת רִבְבוֹת עַמְּךָ בֵּית יִשְׂרָאֵל, בְּרִנָּה יִתְפָּאַר שִׁמְךָ מַלְכֵּנוּ בְּכָל דּוֹר וָדוֹר, שֶׁכֵּן חוֹבַת כָּל הַיְצוּרִים לְפָנֶיךָ יהוה אֱלֹהֵינוּ וֵאלֹהֵי אֲבוֹתֵינוּ, לְהוֹדוֹת לְהַלֵּל לְשַׁבֵּחַ לְפָאֵר לְרוֹמֵם לְהַדֵּר לְבָרֵךְ לְעַלֵּה וּלְקַלֵּס, עַל כָּל דִּבְרֵי שִׁירוֹת וְתִשְׁבְּחוֹת דָּוִד בֶּן יִשַׁי עַבְדְּךָ מְשִׁיחֶךָ:

יִשְׁתַּבַּח שִׁמְךָ לָעַד מַלְכֵּנוּ, הָאֵל הַמֶּלֶךְ הַגָּדוֹל וְהַקָּדוֹשׁ בַּשָּׁמַיִם וּבָאָרֶץ, כִּי לְךָ נָאֶה יהוה אֱלֹהֵינוּ וֵאלֹהֵי אֲבוֹתֵינוּ, שִׁיר וּשְׁבָחָה הַלֵּל וְזִמְרָה עֹז וּמֶמְשָׁלָה נֶצַח גְּדֻלָּה וּגְבוּרָה תְּהִלָּה וְתִפְאֶרֶת קְדֻשָּׁה וּמַלְכוּת בְּרָכוֹת וְהוֹדָאוֹת מֵעַתָּה וְעַד עוֹלָם, בָּרוּךְ אַתָּה יהוה מֶלֶךְ מְהֻלָּל בַּתִּשְׁבָּחוֹת:

בָּרוּךְ אַתָּה יהוה אֱלֹהֵינוּ מֶלֶךְ הָעוֹלָם, בּוֹרֵא פְּרִי הַגָּפֶן:

The fourth cup of wine is now drunk, while reclining on the left side.

God—in the might of Your strength; great in the glory of Your Name; mighty forever; and awesome in Your awesome deeds; the King Who sits upon an exalted and lofty throne. He abides forever, exalted and holy is His Name. And it is written: "Shout out with joy to Hashem, you righteous ones; it is befitting for the upright to offer praise" (Tehillim 33:1). By the mouth of the upright You shall be praised; by the words of the righteous You shall be blessed; by the tongue of the pious You shall be exalted; and among the holy ones You shall be sanctified.

AND in the assemblies of the myriads of Your People, the House of Israel, Your name shall be glorified with joyful shouts, our King, in every generation. For this is the duty of all creatures before You, Hashem, our God and God of our fathers—to thank, to praise, to laud, to glorify, to exalt, to honor, to bless, to elevate and to extol [You], even beyond all the words of song and praise of David son of Jesse, Your anointed servant. May Your Name be praised forever, our King, the God and King Who is great and holy in heaven and on earth. For to You, Hashem, our God and God of our fathers, are befitting song and praise, laud and hymn, strength and dominion, eternity, greatness and might, glorification and splendor, holiness and sovereignty, blessings and thanksgiving—for all eternity.

BLESSED are You, Hashem, God, King, great in praises, God of thanksgiving, Lord of wonders, Who favors melodious songs of praise, the King, the Life of the universe.

Blessed are You, Hashem, our God, King of the universe, who creates the fruit of the vine.

The fourth cup of wine is now drunk, while reclining on the left side.

After drinking the fourth cup, the following blessing is said:
(On Shabbos, the words in parentheses are added.)

בָּרוּךְ אַתָּה יהוה אֱלֹהֵינוּ מֶלֶךְ הָעוֹלָם, עַל הַגֶּפֶן וְעַל פְּרִי
הַגֶּפֶן וְעַל תְּנוּבַת הַשָּׂדֶה וְעַל אֶרֶץ חֶמְדָּה טוֹבָה וּרְחָבָה,
שֶׁרָצִיתָ וְהִנְחַלְתָּ לַאֲבוֹתֵינוּ, לֶאֱכֹל מִפִּרְיָהּ וְלִשְׂבֹּעַ מִטּוּבָהּ.
רַחֶם (נָא) יהוה אֱלֹהֵינוּ עַל יִשְׂרָאֵל עַמֶּךָ, וְעַל יְרוּשָׁלַיִם
עִירֶךָ, וְעַל צִיּוֹן מִשְׁכַּן כְּבוֹדֶךָ וְעַל מִזְבְּחֶךָ וְעַל הֵיכָלֶךָ.
וּבְנֵה יְרוּשָׁלַיִם עִיר הַקֹּדֶשׁ בִּמְהֵרָה בְיָמֵינוּ, וְהַעֲלֵנוּ לְתוֹכָהּ
וְשַׂמְּחֵנוּ בְּבִנְיָנָהּ וְנֹאכַל מִפִּרְיָהּ וְנִשְׂבַּע מִטּוּבָהּ, וּנְבָרֶכְךָ
עָלֶיהָ בִּקְדֻשָּׁה וּבְטָהֳרָה, (וּרְצֵה וְהַחֲלִיצֵנוּ בְּיוֹם הַשַּׁבָּת
הַזֶּה) וְשַׂמְּחֵנוּ בְּיוֹם חַג הַמַּצּוֹת הַזֶּה כִּי אַתָּה יהוה טוֹב
וּמֵטִיב לַכֹּל, וְנוֹדֶה לְּךָ עַל הָאָרֶץ וְעַל פְּרִי הַגָּפֶן: בָּרוּךְ
אַתָּה יהוה, עַל הָאָרֶץ וְעַל פְּרִי הַגָּפֶן:

נרצה

חֲסַל סִדּוּר פֶּסַח כְּהִלְכָתוֹ, כְּכָל מִשְׁפָּטוֹ וְחֻקָּתוֹ, כַּאֲשֶׁר זָכִינוּ
לְסַדֵּר אוֹתוֹ, כֵּן נִזְכֶּה לַעֲשׂוֹתוֹ, זָךְ שׁוֹכֵן מְעוֹנָה, קוֹמֵם קְהַל
עֲדַת מִי מָנָה, בְּקָרוֹב נַהֵל נִטְעֵי כַנָּה, פְּדוּיִם לְצִיּוֹן בְּרִנָּה.

לְשָׁנָה הַבָּאָה בִּירוּשָׁלָיִם!

חֲסַל סִדּוּר פֶּסַח כְּהִלְכָתוֹ, *we have finished performing all the detailed
laws of the Pesach Seder. Why do we use the Aramaic word* חֲסַל?

So that the guests (who were more fluent in the commonly spoken
Aramaic) would understand that the Seder was over, and they could
go home at this point if they wanted (*Haggadas Marbeh Lesaper*).

BLESSED *are You, Hashem our God, King of the universe, for the vine and the fruit of the vine, for the produce of the field, and for the precious, good, and spacious land that You saw fit to grant as a possession to our fathers, to eat of its fruit and be sated by its goodness. Have mercy, Hashem our God, on Israel Your People, on Jerusalem Your city, on Zion the abode of Your glory, on Your altar, and on Your Temple. Rebuild Jerusalem, the holy city, speedily in our days, and bring us up into it and let us rejoice in its rebuilding; let us partake of its fruits and be sated by its goodness, and bless You upon it in holiness and purity. (May it please You to grant us strength on this Sabbath day) and remember us for good on this day of the Festival of Matzos. For You, Hashem, are benevolent and bestow benevolence upon all, and we give thanks to You for the land and for the fruit of the vine.*

Blessed are You, Hashem, for the land and for the fruit of the vine.

NIRTZAH

THIS *is the completion of the Pesach ceremony according to its rules, In accordance with all its laws and statutes. Just as we merited to present it, So may we merit to perform it. Pure One, Who dwells on high, Raise up the congregation of whom it was said, "Who can count them?" (Bamidbar 23:10)! Soon lead the plants of your vineyard (Israel), Redeemed, to Zion, with shouts of joy.*

NEXT YEAR IN JERUSALEM!

Which word in נִרְצָה did the Brisker Rav object to saying?

The Brisker Rav objected to saying הַבְּנוּיָה in לְשָׁנָה הַבָּאָה בִּירוּשָׁלַיִם הַבְּנוּיָה, *next year in the rebuilt Yerushalayim,* since there is no early source for adding this to the standard לְשָׁנָה הַבָּאָה בִּירוּשָׁלָיִם (*Haggadah Mi'Beis Levi*).

וּבְכֵן וַיְהִי בַּחֲצִי הַלַּיְלָה:

בַּלַּיְלָה.   אָז רוֹב נִסִּים הִפְלֵאתָ

הַלַּיְלָה.   בְּרֹאשׁ אַשְׁמוֹרֶת זֶה

לַיְלָה.   גֵּר צֶדֶק נִצַּחְתּוֹ כְּנֶחֱלַק לוֹ

וַיְהִי בַּחֲצִי הַלַּיְלָה:

הַלַּיְלָה.   דַּנְתָּ מֶלֶךְ גְּרָר בַּחֲלוֹם

לַיְלָה.   הִפְחַדְתָּ אֲרַמִּי בְּאֶמֶשׁ

לַיְלָה.   וַיָּשַׂר יִשְׂרָאֵל לְמַלְאָךְ וַיּוּכַל לוֹ

וַיְהִי בַּחֲצִי הַלַּיְלָה:

הַלַּיְלָה.   זֶרַע בְּכוֹרֵי פַּתְרוֹס מָחַצְתָּ בַּחֲצִי

בַּלַּיְלָה.   חֵילָם לֹא מָצְאוּ בְּקוּמָם

לַיְלָה.   טִיסַת נְגִיד חֲרוֹשֶׁת סִלִּיתָ בְּכוֹכְבֵי

וַיְהִי בַּחֲצִי הַלַּיְלָה:

בַּלַּיְלָה.   יָעַץ מְחָרֵף לְנוֹפֵף אִוּוּי הוֹבַשְׁתָּ פְגָרָיו

לַיְלָה.   כָּרַע בֵּל וּמַצָּבוֹ בְּאִישׁוֹן

When did Avraham Avinu earn the title
גֵּר צֶדֶק, righteous convert?

We say in this *piyut* that the גֵּר צֶדֶק won the battle at midnight. This is a reference to Avraham Avinu, who was thrown into the fire by Nimrod

This poem is recited on the first night:

"It happened at midnight" (Shemos 12:29)

Always, You have performed wondrous miracles on this night.

At the beginning of the watches on this night,

You granted victory to the righteous convert (Avraham) when the night was divided in two (Bereishis 14:15).

It happened at midnight.

You judged the king of Gerar (Avimelech) in a dream at night (ibid. 20:3).

You frightened the Aramean (Lavan) in the dark of the night (ibid. 31:24).

Israel struggled with an angel and overcame him at night (ibid. 32:25)

It happened at midnight.

You crushed the firstborn offspring of Pathros (Egypt) at midnight.

They did not find their vigor (firstborn sons) when they awoke in the middle of the night.

You trampled the swift army of the Prince of Harosheth (Sisera) by the stars of the night (Shoftim 5:20).

It happened at midnight.

The blasphemer (Sancheriv) planned to wave his hand against the cherished Temple; You dried out his corpses overnight (II Melachim 19:35).

and was subsequently miraculously saved, on the night of Pesach. It was at this point in Avraham Avinu's life that he earned himself the title גֵר צֶדֶק (*Abarbanel*).

לְאִישׁ חֲמוּדוֹת נִגְלָה רָז חֲזוֹת לַיְלָה.
וַיְהִי בַּחֲצִי הַלַּיְלָה:

מִשְׁתַּכֵּר בִּכְלֵי קֹדֶשׁ נֶהֱרַג בּוֹ בַּלַּיְלָה.
נוֹשַׁע מִבּוֹר אֲרָיוֹת פּוֹתֵר בְּעִתּוּתֵי לַיְלָה.
שִׂנְאָה נָטַר אֲגָגִי וְכָתַב סְפָרִים בַּלַּיְלָה.
וַיְהִי בַּחֲצִי הַלַּיְלָה:

עוֹרַרְתָּ נִצְחֲךָ עָלָיו בְּנֶדֶד שְׁנַת לַיְלָה.
פּוּרָה תִדְרוֹךְ לְשׁוֹמֵר מַה מִלַּיְלָה.
צָרַח כַּשּׁוֹמֵר וְשָׂח אָתָא בֹקֶר וְגַם לַיְלָה.
וַיְהִי בַּחֲצִי הַלַּיְלָה:

קָרֵב יוֹם אֲשֶׁר הוּא לֹא יוֹם וְלֹא לַיְלָה.
רָם הוֹדַע כִּי לְךָ הַיּוֹם אַף לְךָ הַלַּיְלָה.
שׁוֹמְרִים הַפְקֵד לְעִירְךָ כָּל הַיּוֹם וְכָל הַלַּיְלָה.
תָּאִיר כְּאוֹר יוֹם חֶשְׁכַּת לַיְלָה.
וַיְהִי בַּחֲצִי הַלַּיְלָה:

〰〰

Bel (Babylonia) and its watchmen collapsed in the dark of night;

To the beloved man (Daniel) was revealed the secret of the vision at night (Daniel 5).

It happened at midnight.

The one who became drunk drinking from the sacred vessels (Belshazzar) was killed that very night (ibid.).

The one saved from the lion's den (Daniel) interpreted the frightening sight at night (ibid.).

The Agagite (Haman) retained his hatred and wrote writs at night (Esther 5:14–6:4).

It happened at midnight.

You launched Your triumph against him (Haman) when [Achashveirosh's] sleep was disturbed at night (ibid.).

You will trample the vintage of the one (Edom) of whom it was said, "Watchman, what of the night?" (Yeshayahu 21:11).

God shouted back like a watchman and said, "Morning is coming, but also night" (ibid. 21:12).

It happened at midnight.

Bring near the day (of the Messiah) which is "neither day nor night" (Zechariah 14:7).

Exalted One, make it known that "Yours is the day and Yours is the night" (Tehillim 74:16).

Post guardians over Your city all day and all night (Yeshayahu 61:6).

Light up the dark of night as brightly as the light of day.

It happened at midnight.

וּבְכֵן וַאֲמַרְתֶּם זֶבַח פֶּסַח:

בְּפֶסַח. אֹמֶץ גְּבוּרוֹתֶיךָ הִפְלֵאתָ

פֶּסַח. בְּרֹאשׁ כָּל מוֹעֲדוֹת נִשֵּׂאתָ

פֶּסַח. גִּלִּיתָ לְאֶזְרָחִי חֲצוֹת לֵיל

וַאֲמַרְתֶּם זֶבַח פֶּסַח:

בְּפֶסַח. דְּלָתָיו דָּפַקְתָּ כְּחוֹם הַיּוֹם

בְּפֶסַח. הִסְעִיד נוֹצְצִים עֻגּוֹת מַצּוֹת

פֶּסַח. וְאֶל הַבָּקָר רָץ זֵכֶר לְשׁוֹר עֵרֶךְ

וַאֲמַרְתֶּם זֶבַח פֶּסַח:

בְּפֶסַח. זֹעֲמוּ סְדוֹמִים וְלֹהֲטוּ בָּאֵשׁ

פֶּסַח. חֻלַּץ לוֹט מֵהֶם וּמַצּוֹת אָפָה בְּקֵץ

בְּפֶסַח. טֵאטֵאתָ אַדְמַת מוֹף וְנוֹף בְּעָבְרְךָ

וַאֲמַרְתֶּם זֶבַח פֶּסַח:

פֶּסַח. יָהּ רֹאשׁ כָּל אוֹן מָחַצְתָּ בְּלֵיל שִׁמּוּר

פֶּסַח. כַּבִּיר עַל בֵּן בְּכוֹר פָּסַחְתָּ בְּדַם

בְּפֶסַח. לְבִלְתִּי תֵּת מַשְׁחִית לָבֹא בִּפְתָחַי

וַאֲמַרְתֶּם זֶבַח פֶּסַח:

פֶּסַח. מִסְגֶּרֶת סֻגְּרָה בְּעִתּוֹתֵי

פֶּסַח. נִשְׁמְדָה מִדְיָן בִּצְלִיל שְׂעוֹרֵי עֹמֶר

*And you shall say, "It is a sacrifice of Pesach" (Shemos 12:27).
You demonstrated the power of Your might on Pesach. You elevated as the first of the holidays, Pesach (Vayikra 23:4–5). You revealed to the Easterner (Avraham) the events of the midnight of Pesach.*

And you shall say, "It is a sacrifice of Pesach."

You knocked on his (Avraham's) door in the heat of the day on Pesach (Bereishis 18:1); He fed angels unleavened cakes on Pesach (ibid. 18:6); He ran to take from the cattle (ibid. 18:7), symbolizing the ox brought in conjunction with the sacrifice of Pesach.

And you shall say, "It is a sacrifice of Pesach."

The Sodomites were damned and burnt in fire on Pesach. Lot was rescued from among them; he baked unleavened bread (ibid. 19:3) at the end of the eve of Pesach. You wiped out the land of Moph and Noph (Egypt) when You passed through on Pesach.

And you shall say, "It is a sacrifice of Pesach."

God, You crushed the first one of all their child-bearing, on the "night of watching" (Shemos 12:42) of Pesach. Mighty One, You passed over [Your own] firstborn son because of the blood of the Pesach, Not allowing the Destroyer to enter my doors on Pesach.

And you shall say, "It is a sacrifice of Pesach."

The sealed city (Jericho) was handed over during the time of Pesach. Midian was destroyed through a loaf representing the barley of the Omer sacrifice of Pesach (Shoftim 7:13). The burly

שׁוֹרְפוּ מִשְׁמַנֵּי פוּל וְלוּד בִּיקַד יְקוֹד   פֶּסַח.

וַאֲמַרְתֶּם זֶבַח פֶּסַח:

עוֹד הַיּוֹם בְּנוֹב לַעֲמוֹד עַד גָּעָה עוֹנַת   פֶּסַח.

פַּס יָד כָּתְבָה לְקַעֲקֵעַ צוּל   בְּפֶסַח.

צָפֹה הַצָּפִית עָרוֹךְ הַשֻּׁלְחָן   בְּפֶסַח.

וַאֲמַרְתֶּם זֶבַח פֶּסַח:

קָהָל כִּנְּסָה הֲדַסָּה צוֹם לְשַׁלֵּשׁ   בְּפֶסַח.

רֹאשׁ מִבֵּית רָשָׁע מָחַצְתָּ בְּעֵץ חֲמִשִּׁים   בְּפֶסַח.

שְׁתֵּי אֵלֶּה רֶגַע תָּבִיא לְעוּצִית   בְּפֶסַח.

תָּעֹז יָדְךָ וְתָרוּם יְמִינְךָ כְּלֵיל הִתְקַדֶּשׁ חַג   פֶּסַח.

וַאֲמַרְתֶּם זֶבַח פֶּסַח:

〜〜〜

כִּי לוֹ נָאֶה, כִּי לוֹ יָאֶה.

אַדִּיר בִּמְלוּכָה, בָּחוּר כַּהֲלָכָה, גְּדוּדָיו יֹאמְרוּ לוֹ.

לְךָ וּלְךָ, לְךָ כִּי לְךָ, לְךָ אַף לְךָ, לְךָ יְיָ הַמַּמְלָכָה, כִּי לוֹ נָאֶה, כִּי לוֹ יָאֶה.

דָּגוּל בִּמְלוּכָה, הָדוּר כַּהֲלָכָה, וָתִיקָיו יֹאמְרוּ לוֹ.

לְךָ וּלְךָ, לְךָ כִּי לְךָ, לְךָ אַף לְךָ, לְךָ יְיָ הַמַּמְלָכָה, כִּי לוֹ נָאֶה, כִּי לוֹ יָאֶה.

warriors of Pul and Lud (Assyria) were burnt in a conflagration on Pesach (Yeshayahu 10:16).

And you shall say, "It is a sacrifice of Pesach."

He (Sancheriv) wanted "to reach Nob that very day" (ibid. 10:32)—until it became the season of Pesach. The palm of a hand wrote an inscription about the crushing of the well-watered country (Babylonia) on Pesach; "The chandelier was lit and table was set" (ibid. 21:5, describing the downfall of Babylonia) on Pesach.

And you shall say, "It is a sacrifice of Pesach."

Hadassah assembled the congregation to hold a three-day fast on Pesach (Esther 4:16). You vanquished the chief (Haman) from the wicked family (Amalek) on a fifty-cubit wooden pole on Pesach. May You bring "these two things" (Yeshayahu 47:9) in an instant upon the Utzites (Babylonians) on Pesach! Let Your hand be strong and Your right hand raised, as on the night of the sanctification of the holiday of Pesach!

And you shall say, "It is a sacrifice of Pesach."

To Him it is befitting! To Him it is becoming!

Mighty in dominion, Superior indeed, His legions (angels) say to Him: To You, to You! To You, indeed to You! To You, only to You! To You, Hashem, belongs the dominion (I Divrei Hayamim 29:11)!

To Him it is befitting! To Him it is becoming!

Outstanding in dominion, Glorious indeed, His devoted ones (Israel) say to Him: To You, to You! To You, indeed to You! To You, only to You! To You, Hashem, belongs the dominion!

זַכַּאי בִּמְלוּכָה, חָסִין כַּהֲלָכָה, טַפְסְרָיו יֹאמְרוּ לוֹ.
לְךָ וּלְךָ, לְךָ כִּי לְךָ, לְךָ אַף לְךָ, לְךָ יְיָ הַמַּמְלָכָה, כִּי לוֹ נָאֶה, כִּי לוֹ יָאֶה.

יָחִיד בִּמְלוּכָה, כַּבִּיר כַּהֲלָכָה, לִמּוּדָיו יֹאמְרוּ לוֹ.
לְךָ וּלְךָ, לְךָ כִּי לְךָ, לְךָ אַף לְךָ, לְךָ יְיָ הַמַּמְלָכָה, כִּי לוֹ נָאֶה, כִּי לוֹ יָאֶה.

מוֹשֵׁל בִּמְלוּכָה, נוֹרָא כַּהֲלָכָה, סְבִיבָיו יֹאמְרוּ לוֹ.
לְךָ וּלְךָ, לְךָ כִּי לְךָ, לְךָ אַף לְךָ, לְךָ יְיָ הַמַּמְלָכָה, כִּי לוֹ נָאֶה, כִּי לוֹ יָאֶה.

עָנָיו בִּמְלוּכָה, פּוֹדֶה כַּהֲלָכָה, צַדִּיקָיו יֹאמְרוּ לוֹ.
לְךָ וּלְךָ, לְךָ כִּי לְךָ, לְךָ אַף לְךָ, לְךָ יְיָ הַמַּמְלָכָה, כִּי לוֹ נָאֶה, כִּי לוֹ יָאֶה.

קָדוֹשׁ בִּמְלוּכָה, רַחוּם כַּהֲלָכָה, שִׁנְאַנָּיו יֹאמְרוּ לוֹ.
לְךָ וּלְךָ, לְךָ כִּי לְךָ, לְךָ אַף לְךָ, לְךָ יְיָ הַמַּמְלָכָה, כִּי לוֹ נָאֶה, כִּי לוֹ יָאֶה.

תַּקִּיף בִּמְלוּכָה, תּוֹמֵךְ כַּהֲלָכָה, תְּמִימָיו יֹאמְרוּ לוֹ.
לְךָ וּלְךָ, לְךָ כִּי לְךָ, לְךָ אַף לְךָ, לְךָ יְיָ הַמַּמְלָכָה, כִּי לוֹ נָאֶה, כִּי לוֹ יָאֶה.

To Him it is befitting! To Him it is becoming!

Pure in dominion, Powerful indeed, His captains (angels) say to Him: To You, to You! To You, indeed to You! To You, only to You! To You, Hashem, belongs the dominion!

To Him it is befitting! To Him it is becoming!

Unique in dominion, Potent indeed, His learned ones (Israel) say to Him: To You, to You! To You, indeed to You! To You, only to You! To You, Hashem, belongs the dominion!

To Him it is befitting! To Him it is becoming!

Exalted in dominion, Awesome indeed, those surrounding Him (angels) say to Him: To You, to You! To You, indeed to You! To You, only to You! To You, Hashem, belongs the dominion!

To Him it is befitting! To Him it is becoming!

Deigning in dominion, Redeeming indeed, His righteous ones (Israel) say to Him: To You, to You! To You, indeed to You! To You, only to You! To You, Hashem, belongs the dominion!

To Him it is befitting! To Him it is becoming!

Holy in dominion, Compassionate indeed, His Shinanim (angels) say to Him: To You, to You! To You, indeed to You! To You, only to You! To You, Hashem, belongs the dominion!

To Him it is befitting! To Him it is becoming!

Strong in dominion, Supporter indeed, His faithful ones (Israel) say to Him: To You, to You! To You, indeed to You! To You, only to You! To You, Hashem, belongs the dominion!

To Him it is befitting! To Him it is becoming!

אַדִּיר הוּא יִבְנֶה בֵּיתוֹ בְּקָרוֹב, בִּמְהֵרָה בִּמְהֵרָה בְּיָמֵינוּ בְּקָרוֹב, אֵל בְּנֵה אֵל בְּנֵה, בְּנֵה בֵיתְךָ בְּקָרוֹב.

בָּחוּר הוּא, גָּדוֹל הוּא, דָּגוּל הוּא, יִבְנֶה בֵּיתוֹ בְּקָרוֹב. בִּמְהֵרָה בִּמְהֵרָה בְּיָמֵינוּ בְּקָרוֹב, אֵל בְּנֵה אֵל בְּנֵה, בְּנֵה בֵיתְךָ בְּקָרוֹב.

הָדוּר הוּא, וָתִיק הוּא, זַכַּאי הוּא, חָסִיד הוּא, יִבְנֶה בֵּיתוֹ בְּקָרוֹב, בִּמְהֵרָה בְּיָמֵינוּ בְּקָרוֹב, אֵל בְּנֵה אֵל בְּנֵה, בְּנֵה בֵיתְךָ בְּקָרוֹב.

טָהוֹר הוּא, יָחִיד הוּא, כַּבִּיר הוּא, לָמוּד הוּא, מֶלֶךְ הוּא, נוֹרָא הוּא, סַגִּיב הוּא, עִזּוּז הוּא, פּוֹדֶה הוּא, צַדִּיק הוּא, יִבְנֶה בֵּיתוֹ בְּקָרוֹב, בִּמְהֵרָה בִּמְהֵרָה בְּיָמֵינוּ בְּקָרוֹב, אֵל בְּנֵה אֵל בְּנֵה, בְּנֵה בֵיתְךָ בְּקָרוֹב.

קָדוֹשׁ הוּא, רַחוּם הוּא, שַׁדַּי הוּא, תַּקִּיף הוּא, יִבְנֶה בֵּיתוֹ בְּקָרוֹב, בִּמְהֵרָה בִּמְהֵרָה בְּיָמֵינוּ בְּקָרוֹב, אֵל בְּנֵה אֵל בְּנֵה, בְּנֵה בֵיתְךָ בְּקָרוֹב.

According to the Chasam Sofer, which statement in אַדִּיר הוּא should not be said?

Saying לָמוּד הוּא, *He is being taught*, denotes that Hashem learns from others. Since Hashem is the Source of all knowledge, saying that Hashem learns from others is considered blasphemous. Rather, one should say לוֹחֵם הוּא, indicating that Hashem at times acts like

He is mighty! May He build His Temple soon! Speedily, speedily, in our days, soon! God, build, God build, build Your Temple soon!

He is superior! He is great! He is outstanding!

May He build His Temple soon! Speedily, speedily, in our days, soon! God, build, God build, build Your Temple soon!

He is glorious! He is virtuous! He is blameless! He is kind!

May He build His Temple soon! Speedily, speedily, in our days, soon! God, build, God build, build Your Temple soon!

He is pure! He is unique! He is powerful! He is all-knowing! He is King! He is awesome! He is exalted! He is all-powerful! He is the Redeemer! He is righteous!

May He build His Temple soon! Speedily, speedily, in our days, soon! God, build, God build, build Your Temple soon!

He is holy! He is compassionate! He is the Almighty! He is strong!

May He build His Temple soon! Speedily, speedily, in our days, soon! God, build, God build, build Your Temple soon!

a warrior in battle (like we find in *Shemos* 15:3) (*Chasam Sofer* to *Shulchan Aruch* 480:1). Different approaches explain our text of לָמוּד הוּא. Some change the vowels to read לִמוּד הוּא, *Hashem is the knowledge Himself.* Others take issue with the contention that לָמוּד הוּא implies learning from others; rather, they say it means that Hashem is learned, and therefore there is no problem with saying it (see *Otzros HaHaggadah*, p. 811).

אֶחָד מִי יוֹדֵעַ, אֶחָד אֲנִי יוֹדֵעַ, אֶחָד אֱלֹהֵינוּ שֶׁבַּשָּׁמַיִם וּבָאָרֶץ.

שְׁנַיִם מִי יוֹדֵעַ, שְׁנַיִם אֲנִי יוֹדֵעַ. שְׁנֵי לוּחוֹת הַבְּרִית, אֶחָד אֱלֹהֵינוּ שֶׁבַּשָּׁמַיִם וּבָאָרֶץ.

שְׁלֹשָׁה מִי יוֹדֵעַ, שְׁלֹשָׁה אֲנִי יוֹדֵעַ, שְׁלֹשָׁה אָבוֹת, שְׁנֵי לוּחוֹת הַבְּרִית, אֶחָד אֱלֹהֵינוּ שֶׁבַּשָּׁמַיִם וּבָאָרֶץ.

אַרְבַּע מִי יוֹדֵעַ, אַרְבַּע אֲנִי יוֹדֵעַ, אַרְבַּע אִמָּהוֹת, שְׁלֹשָׁה אָבוֹת, שְׁנֵי לוּחוֹת הַבְּרִית, אֶחָד אֱלֹהֵינוּ שֶׁבַּשָּׁמַיִם וּבָאָרֶץ.

חֲמִשָּׁה מִי יוֹדֵעַ, חֲמִשָּׁה אֲנִי יוֹדֵעַ, חֲמִשָּׁה חוּמְשֵׁי תוֹרָה, אַרְבַּע אִמָּהוֹת, שְׁלֹשָׁה אָבוֹת, שְׁנֵי לוּחוֹת הַבְּרִית, אֶחָד אֱלֹהֵינוּ שֶׁבַּשָּׁמַיִם וּבָאָרֶץ.

Why do we mention תִּשְׁעָה יַרְחֵי לֵידָה, the nine months of pregnancy, at the Seder?

The night of the Seder is a time when we express our *emunah* in Hashem and His Torah. The Rambam (*Moreh Nevuchim* 2:17) tells the following *mashal*: There was once a young boy on an island whose mother passed away when he was yet a baby. Throughout his entire childhood, he never saw a woman. When his father explained to him that all people are nurtured for nine months inside their mother before being born, the boy found the whole idea ridiculous. *After all*, he reasoned, *how can anyone live inside another human being for even a short time, let alone for nine months?! If one were to swallow a live bird, the bird would not be able to live inside the*

Who knows one? I know one!

One is our God, in heaven and on earth.

Who knows two? I know two!

Two are the tablets of the Covenant; One is our God, in heaven and on earth.

Who knows three? I know three!

Three are the patriarchs; two are the tablets of the Covenant; One is our God, in heaven and on earth.

Who knows four? I know four!

Four are the matriarchs; three are the patriarchs; two are the tablets of the Covenant; One is our God, in heaven and on earth.

Who knows five? I know five!

FIVE are the books of the Torah; four are the matriarchs; three are the patriarchs; two are the tablets of the Covenant; One is our God, in heaven and on earth.

person's stomach! Moreover, where would a fetus obtain food and drink from to stay alive for nine months? It just does not make sense, argued the boy.

We understand that one who has never seen otherwise cannot comprehend how a baby is nurtured before it is born. In the same way, we can't fully grasp all of creation's complexities. But just like we know that there are תִּשְׁעָה יַרְחֵי לֵידָה, so too we have *emunah* in the tradition passed down to us from all our ancestors, including Moshe Rabbeinu and Avraham Avinu, that אֶחָד אֱלֹקֵינוּ שֶׁבַּשָּׁמַיִם וּבָאָרֶץ—and our *emunah* in Hashem is unwavering (*Haggadas Leil Shimurim*).

שִׁשָּׁה מִי יוֹדֵעַ, שִׁשָּׁה אֲנִי יוֹדֵעַ, שִׁשָּׁה סִדְרֵי מִשְׁנָה, חֲמִשָּׁה חוּמְשֵׁי תוֹרָה, אַרְבַּע אִמָּהוֹת, שְׁלֹשָׁה אָבוֹת, שְׁנֵי לוּחוֹת הַבְּרִית, אֶחָד אֱלֹהֵינוּ שֶׁבַּשָּׁמַיִם וּבָאָרֶץ.

שִׁבְעָה מִי יוֹדֵעַ, שִׁבְעָה אֲנִי יוֹדֵעַ, שִׁבְעָה יְמֵי שַׁבַּתָּא, שִׁשָּׁה סִדְרֵי מִשְׁנָה, חֲמִשָּׁה חוּמְשֵׁי תוֹרָה, אַרְבַּע אִמָּהוֹת, שְׁלֹשָׁה אָבוֹת, שְׁנֵי לוּחוֹת הַבְּרִית, אֶחָד אֱלֹהֵינוּ שֶׁבַּשָּׁמַיִם וּבָאָרֶץ.

שְׁמוֹנָה מִי יוֹדֵעַ, שְׁמוֹנָה אֲנִי יוֹדֵעַ, שְׁמוֹנָה יְמֵי מִילָה, שִׁבְעָה יְמֵי שַׁבַּתָּא, שִׁשָּׁה סִדְרֵי מִשְׁנָה, חֲמִשָּׁה חוּמְשֵׁי תוֹרָה, אַרְבַּע אִמָּהוֹת, שְׁלֹשָׁה אָבוֹת, שְׁנֵי לוּחוֹת הַבְּרִית, אֶחָד אֱלֹהֵינוּ שֶׁבַּשָּׁמַיִם וּבָאָרֶץ.

תִּשְׁעָה מִי יוֹדֵעַ, תִּשְׁעָה אֲנִי יוֹדֵעַ, תִּשְׁעָה יַרְחֵי לֵידָה, שְׁמוֹנָה יְמֵי מִילָה, שִׁבְעָה יְמֵי שַׁבַּתָּא, שִׁשָּׁה סִדְרֵי מִשְׁנָה, חֲמִשָּׁה חוּמְשֵׁי תוֹרָה, אַרְבַּע אִמָּהוֹת, שְׁלֹשָׁה אָבוֹת, שְׁנֵי לוּחוֹת הַבְּרִית, אֶחָד אֱלֹהֵינוּ שֶׁבַּשָּׁמַיִם וּבָאָרֶץ.

עֲשָׂרָה מִי יוֹדֵעַ, עֲשָׂרָה אֲנִי יוֹדֵעַ, עֲשָׂרָה דִבְּרַיָּא, תִּשְׁעָה יַרְחֵי לֵידָה, שְׁמוֹנָה יְמֵי מִילָה, שִׁבְעָה יְמֵי שַׁבַּתָּא, שִׁשָּׁה סִדְרֵי מִשְׁנָה, חֲמִשָּׁה חוּמְשֵׁי תוֹרָה, אַרְבַּע אִמָּהוֹת, שְׁלֹשָׁה אָבוֹת, שְׁנֵי לוּחוֹת הַבְּרִית, אֶחָד אֱלֹהֵינוּ שֶׁבַּשָּׁמַיִם וּבָאָרֶץ.

Who knows six? I know six!

SIX *are the volumes of the Mishnah; five are the books of the Torah; four are the matriarchs; three are the patriarchs; two are the tablets of the Covenant; One is our God, in heaven and on earth.*

Who knows seven? I know seven!

SEVEN *are the days of the week; six are the volumes of the Mishnah; five are the books of the Torah; four are the matriarchs; three are the patriarchs; two are the tablets of the Covenant; One is our God, in heaven and on earth.*

Who knows eight? I know eight!

EIGHT *are the days until circumcision; seven are the days of the week; six are the volumes of the Mishnah; five are the books of the Torah; four are the matriarchs; three are the patriarchs; two are the tablets of the Covenant; One is our God, in heaven and on earth.*

Who knows nine? I know nine!

NINE *are the months of pregnancy; eight are the days until circumcision; seven are the days of the week; six are the volumes of the Mishnah; five are the books of the Torah; four are the matriarchs; three are the patriarchs; two are the tablets of the Covenant; One is our God, in heaven and on earth.*

Who knows ten? I know ten!

TEN *are the Commandments; nine are the months of pregnancy; eight are the days until circumcision; seven are the days of the week; six are the volumes of the Mishnah; five are the books of the Torah; four are the matriarchs; three are the patriarchs; two are the tablets of the Covenant; One is our God, in heaven and on earth.*

אֶחָד עָשָׂר מִי יוֹדֵעַ, אֶחָד עָשָׂר אֲנִי יוֹדֵעַ, אֶחָד עָשָׂר
כּוֹכְבַיָּא, עֲשָׂרָה דִּבְּרַיָּא, תִּשְׁעָה יַרְחֵי לֵידָה, שְׁמוֹנָה
יְמֵי מִילָה, שִׁבְעָה יְמֵי שַׁבַּתָּא, שִׁשָּׁה סִדְרֵי מִשְׁנָה,
חֲמִשָּׁה חוּמְשֵׁי תוֹרָה, אַרְבַּע אִמָּהוֹת, שְׁלֹשָׁה אָבוֹת,
שְׁנֵי לוּחוֹת הַבְּרִית, אֶחָד אֱלֹהֵינוּ שֶׁבַּשָּׁמַיִם וּבָאָרֶץ.

שְׁנֵים עָשָׂר מִי יוֹדֵעַ, שְׁנֵים עָשָׂר אֲנִי יוֹדֵעַ, שְׁנֵים עָשָׂר
שִׁבְטַיָּא, אֶחָד עָשָׂר כּוֹכְבַיָּא, עֲשָׂרָה דִּבְּרַיָּא, תִּשְׁעָה יַרְחֵי
לֵידָה, שְׁמוֹנָה יְמֵי מִילָה, שִׁבְעָה יְמֵי שַׁבַּתָּא, שִׁשָּׁה סִדְרֵי
מִשְׁנָה, חֲמִשָּׁה חוּמְשֵׁי תוֹרָה, אַרְבַּע אִמָּהוֹת, שְׁלֹשָׁה
אָבוֹת, שְׁנֵי לוּחוֹת הַבְּרִית, אֶחָד אֱלֹהֵינוּ שֶׁבַּשָּׁמַיִם וּבָאָרֶץ.

שְׁלֹשָׁה עָשָׂר מִי יוֹדֵעַ, שְׁלֹשָׁה עָשָׂר אֲנִי יוֹדֵעַ, שְׁלֹשָׁה
עָשָׂר מִדַּיָּא, שְׁנֵים עָשָׂר שִׁבְטַיָּא, אֶחָד עָשָׂר כּוֹכְבַיָּא,
עֲשָׂרָה דִּבְּרַיָּא, תִּשְׁעָה יַרְחֵי לֵידָה, שְׁמוֹנָה יְמֵי מִילָה,
שִׁבְעָה יְמֵי שַׁבַּתָּא, שִׁשָּׁה סִדְרֵי מִשְׁנָה, חֲמִשָּׁה חוּמְשֵׁי
תוֹרָה, אַרְבַּע אִמָּהוֹת, שְׁלֹשָׁה אָבוֹת, שְׁנֵי לוּחוֹת
הַבְּרִית, אֶחָד אֱלֹהֵינוּ שֶׁבַּשָּׁמַיִם וּבָאָרֶץ.

⚜

חַד גַּדְיָא, חַד גַּדְיָא.

דְּזַבִּין אַבָּא בִּתְרֵי זוּזֵי. חַד גַּדְיָא, חַד גַּדְיָא.

וְאָתָא שׁוּנְרָא, וְאָכְלָה לְגַדְיָא, דְּזַבִּין אַבָּא בִּתְרֵי זוּזֵי.
חַד גַּדְיָא, חַד גַּדְיָא.

Who knows eleven? I know eleven!

ELEVEN *are the stars (of Joseph's dream); ten are the Commandments; nine are the months of pregnancy; eight are the days until circumcision; seven are the days of the week; six are the volumes of the Mishnah; five are the books of the Torah; four are the matriarchs; three are the patriarchs; two are the tablets of the Covenant; One is our God, in heaven and on earth.*

Who knows twelve? I know twelve!

TWELVE *are the tribes of Israel; eleven are the stars (of Joseph's dream); ten are the Commandments; nine are the months of pregnancy; eight are the days until circumcision; seven are the days of the week; six are the volumes of the Mishnah; five are the books of the Torah; four are the matriarchs; three are the patriarchs; two are the tablets of the Covenant; One is our God, in heaven and on earth.*

Who knows thirteen? I know thirteen!

THIRTEEN *are God's attributes of mercy; twelve are the tribes of Israel; eleven are the stars (of Joseph's dream); ten are the Commandments; nine are the months of pregnancy; eight are the days until circumcision; seven are the days of the week; six are the volumes of the Mishnah; five are the books of the Torah; four are the matriarchs; three are the patriarchs; two are the tablets of the Covenant; One is our God, in heaven and on earth.*

One kid, one kid—
THAT *my father bought for two zuzim.*
One kid, one kid.

וְאָתָא כַלְבָּא, וְנָשַׁךְ לְשׁוּנְרָא, דְּאָכְלָה לְגַדְיָא, דְּזַבִּין אַבָּא בִּתְרֵי זוּזֵי. חַד גַּדְיָא, חַד גַּדְיָא.

וְאָתָא חוּטְרָא, וְהִכָּה לְכַלְבָּא, דְּנָשַׁךְ לְשׁוּנְרָא, דְּאָכְלָה לְגַדְיָא, דְּזַבִּין אַבָּא בִּתְרֵי זוּזֵי. חַד גַּדְיָא, חַד גַּדְיָא.

וְאָתָא נוּרָא, וְשָׂרַף לְחוּטְרָא, דְּהִכָּה לְכַלְבָּא, דְּנָשַׁךְ לְשׁוּנְרָא, דְּאָכְלָה לְגַדְיָא, דְּזַבִּין אַבָּא בִּתְרֵי זוּזֵי. חַד גַּדְיָא, חַד גַּדְיָא.

וְאָתָא מַיָּא, וְכָבָה לְנוּרָא, דְּשָׂרַף לְחוּטְרָא, דְּהִכָּה לְכַלְבָּא, דְּנָשַׁךְ לְשׁוּנְרָא, דְּאָכְלָה לְגַדְיָא, דְּזַבִּין אַבָּא בִּתְרֵי זוּזֵי. חַד גַּדְיָא, חַד גַּדְיָא.

וְאָתָא תוֹרָא, וְשָׁתָה לְמַיָּא, דְּכָבָה לְנוּרָא, דְּשָׂרַף לְחוּטְרָא, דְּהִכָּה לְכַלְבָּא, דְּנָשַׁךְ לְשׁוּנְרָא, דְּאָכְלָה לְגַדְיָא, דְּזַבִּין אַבָּא בִּתְרֵי זוּזֵי. חַד גַּדְיָא, חַד גַּדְיָא.

וְאָתָא הַשּׁוֹחֵט, וְשָׁחַט לְתוֹרָא, דְּשָׁתָה לְמַיָּא, דְּכָבָה לְנוּרָא, דְּשָׂרַף לְחוּטְרָא, דְּהִכָּה לְכַלְבָּא, דְּנָשַׁךְ

How can חַד גַּדְיָא cause someone to become excommunicated?

The Chida writes that one who makes לֵיצָנוּת (mockery) of the *piyut* חַד גַּדְיָא, implying that it is just a song for little children and not full of deep wisdom, is deserving of נִדּוּי (excommunication), and, in addition, must pay a fine to benefit the poor people (*Shu"t Chayim Sha'al* 1:28). In fact, we find many different explanations among the commentators as to what exactly this

ALONG *came a cat and ate the kid—that my father bought for two zuzim.*

One kid, one kid.

ALONG *came a dog and bit the cat that ate the kid—that my father bought for two zuzim.*

One kid, one kid.

ALONG *came a stick and hit the dog that bit the cat that ate the kid—that my father bought for two zuzim.*

One kid, one kid.

ALONG *came a fire and burnt the stick that hit the dog that bit the cat that ate the kid—that my father bought for two zuzim.*

One kid, one kid.

ALONG *came water and extinguished the fire that burnt the stick that hit the dog that bit the cat that ate the kid—that my father bought for two zuzim.*

One kid, one kid.

ALONG *came an ox and drank the water that extinguished the fire that burnt the stick that hit the dog that bit the cat that ate the kid—that my father bought for two zuzim.*

One kid, one kid.

ALONG *came the slaughterer and slaughtered the ox that drank the water that extinguished the fire that burnt the stick*

song of חַד גַּדְיָא is referring to. Some say it expresses ideas regarding the exile and redemption from Mitzrayim, others say it conveys thoughts about the Jewish nation's survival among the nations of the world, while still others say it is about the struggle of the soul to remain pure in this world of temptation. All agree, however, that it is a *piyut* full of deep insights.

לְשׁוּנְרָא, דְּאָכְלָה לְגַדְיָא, דְּזַבִּין אַבָּא בִּתְרֵי זוּזֵי. חַד גַּדְיָא, חַד גַּדְיָא.

וְאָתָא מַלְאַךְ הַמָּוֶת, וְשָׁחַט לְשׁוֹחֵט, דְּשָׁחַט לְתוֹרָא, דְּשָׁתָה לְמַיָּא, דְּכָבָה לְנוּרָא, דְּשָׂרַף לְחוּטְרָא, דְּהִכָּה לְכַלְבָּא, דְּנָשַׁךְ לְשׁוּנְרָא, דְּאָכְלָה לְגַדְיָא, דְּזַבִּין אַבָּא בִּתְרֵי זוּזֵי. חַד גַּדְיָא, חַד גַּדְיָא.

וְאָתָא הַקָּדוֹשׁ בָּרוּךְ הוּא, וְשָׁחַט לְמַלְאַךְ הַמָּוֶת, דְּשָׁחַט לְשׁוֹחֵט, דְּשָׁחַט לְתוֹרָא, דְּשָׁתָה לְמַיָּא, דְּכָבָה לְנוּרָא, דְּשָׂרַף לְחוּטְרָא, דְּהִכָּה לְכַלְבָּא, דְּנָשַׁךְ לְשׁוּנְרָא, דְּאָכְלָה לְגַדְיָא, דְּזַבִּין אַבָּא בִּתְרֵי זוּזֵי. חַד גַּדְיָא, חַד גַּדְיָא.

This is the end of the Haggadah, but each person should, to the best of his ability, follow the dictum of the Sages that "whoever expands upon the recounting of the story of the Exodus from Egypt is praiseworthy." Some have the custom of reciting Shir HaShirim after the Seder.

that hit the dog that bit the cat that ate the kid—that my fa-
ther bought for two zuzim.

One kid, one kid.

ALONG *came the angel of death and killed the slaughterer who*
slaughtered the ox that drank the water that extinguished the
fire that burnt the stick that hit the dog that bit the cat that ate
the kid—that my father bought for two zuzim.

One kid, one kid.

THEN *came the Holy One, Blessed is He and killed the angel of*
death who killed the slaughterer who slaughtered the ox that
drank the water that extinguished the fire that burnt the stick
that hit the dog that bit the cat that ate the kid—that my fa-
ther bought for two zuzim.

One kid, one kid.

This is the end of the Haggadah, but each person should, to the best of his ability, follow
the dictum of the Sages that "whoever expands upon the recounting of the story of the
Exodus from Egypt is praiseworthy." Some have the custom of reciting Shir HaShirim
after the Seder.

ABOUT THE AUTHOR

RABBI A. LEVIN was born and raised in Copenhagen, Denmark, and studied in Ner Israel Rabbinical College in Baltimore under Rabbi Yaakov Weinberg, *zt"l*. He also learned in Yeshivas Heichal Hatorah under Rabbi Tzvi Kushelefsky, as well as in Yeshivas Mir Yerushalayim. He received *semichah* from Rabbi Zalman Nechemia Goldberg in 2002 and moved with his family to join Kollel Beis Hatalmud in Australia, where he learned for seven years. Rabbi Levin took up his current teaching position in 2009 in the high school of Yeshivas Yesodei Hatorah, where he is seen as a warm and dedicated *rebbi* to his *talmidim*. He is known as a talented lecturer in the community, giving *shiurim* and talks in various places around Melbourne. Rabbi Levin is a prominent contributor to several Torah publications and educational forums. In 2012, he won an award from the Chofetz Chaim Heritage Foundation for his curriculum on teaching mitzvos *bein adam l'chaveiro*. This is his first book.

In loving memory of our
beloved grandparents
who gave us
the best of their
Jewish heritage

Meltzer Family

Melbourne, Australia

לעילוי נשמת

ר׳ ישראל בן ר׳ מנחם ז״ל

In loving memory of Mr. Izzy Herzog

Dedicated by the Herzog Family

Dedicated in appreciation of the contribution made by

Rabbi Levin

to *chinuch* in Melbourne, Australia

From
A grateful member of the community

In appreciation to R' Nachman Sofer *shlit"a*
for your dedication and inspirational teaching.
May Hashem bentsch you and your family with all the *brachos*
in *ruchniyus* and *gashmiyus*; health and strength to continue
your *avodas hakodesh* amidst *nachas* and *simchah*.

Lehavdil bein chaim l'chaim

לעילוי נשמת אבי מורי

ר׳ אפרים דב בן ר׳ יוסף חיים הלוי ע״ה

Moishe Landau and Family

ברכת מזל-טוב שלוחה לידי״נ

ר׳ אבא לוין

לרגל הופעת ספרו הראשון והנפלא על הגדה של פסח

תזכה ללכת מחיל אל חיל ויפוצו מעינותיך חוצה

בידידות

משפחת יחיאל בייקער

Warmest Mazel Tov wishes on the publication
of your excellent Haggadah Shel Pesach,
Family Yechiel Baker

Dedicated in memory of our beloved daughter
Dr. Kerry Massel-Arrow

קרן בת חיים

25th Sept 1980–6th Dec 2016.

"To anyone staring down a dream I say this to you:
No matter the disability, challenge, or obstacle,
it can and will happen if you make it so."

(Words of Dr. Kerry Massel-Arrow)

לעילוי נשמת

מו״ה יעקב שלמה בן מו״ה אליעזר הלוי ז״ל

נלב״ע י״א אלול תשס״ז

בילא ע״ה בת מו״ה יוסף יהודה ז״ל

נלב״ע ח׳ שבט תש״נ

ת.נ.צ.ב.ה.